For _____ "_
ed_____ House
students,

_____,
2010

42

Deep Thought on Life, the Universe, and Everything

Mark Vernon

ONEWORLD

OXFORD

A Oneworld Book

Published by Oneworld Publications 2008
Copyright © Mark Vernon 2008

ISBN: 978–1–85168–560–8

Typeset by Jayvee, Trivandrum, India
Cover design by James Nunn
Printed and bound in the United States of America

Oneworld Publications
185 Banbury Road
Oxford OX2 7AR
England
www.oneworld-publications.com

In memory of Richard Butler, who for some time edited
The Referee, a newspaper with the inspiring strapline,
'The paper that makes you think'.

Contents

42: Deep Thought on Life, the Universe, and Everything

THE EVERYDAY LIFE

THE WORKING LIFE

THE EXAMINED LIFE

THE END OF LIFE

Acknowledgements

My great thanks go to Martha Jay and others at Oneworld who have subsequently worked on this book. Since it has no bibliography, I thought I could take the opportunity of this space to mention half a dozen books that I have particularly valued when thinking about the themes that follow, in addition to those explicitly referenced in the essays themselves. In no order: *What is Ancient Philosophy?* by Pierre Hadot (Belknap Press, 2004) is just one of the more recent of his books that explore philosophy as a way of life not just thought; *Sources of the Self: The Making of Modern Identity* by Charles Taylor (Cambridge University Press, 1992) is rich in many ways, not least for its appreciation of religious and philosophical ideas; *After Virtue* by Alasdair McIntyre (University of Notre Dame Press, 1981) is a classic for all interested in virtue ethics; *The Morality of Happiness* by Julia Annas (Oxford University Press, 1995) is a great aid in understanding ancient ethics; *The Fragility of Goodness: Luck and Ethics in Greek Tragedy and Philosophy* by Martha Nussbaum (Cambridge University Press, 2001) is wonderful for its integration of ancient philosophy and literature; *The Use of Pleasure; The History of Sexuality: 2* by Michel Foucault (Penguin Books, 1992) is tremendous for its call to be different.

Introduction

Forty-two, as calculated by the supercomputer Deep Thought in *The Hitchhikers Guide to the Galaxy*, is the answer to life, the Universe and everything. It is, of course, not an answer but a joke. But was it a sad joke – implying that there is, ultimately, no answer? Or was it wisdom – that the answer to life is not found in abstractions like numbers but only in lives actually lived? I reckon Deep Thought was wise. In *42: Deep Thought on Life, the Universe, and Everything*, I will take forty-two aphorisms, written by individuals who have lived life richly, as starting-points for those seeking to live more fully now.

This is no easy matter. Anyone who has tried, for example, to re-adjust their work–life balance knows that. The pretence that making changes in life is straightforward, once you have 'got with the programme' or 'discovered the secret', is why much self-help, albeit well-intended, is disappointing or complacent. *42* tries to cut away the fat and explore what might truly make a difference.

My inspiration is philosophy: not the philosophy of rules or conundrums but the philosophy that asks the question of 'How should I live?' This was how the ancient philosophers understood their subject. Theirs was a philosophy that sought meaning as well as insight, was inspired by practical challenges as well as rational results and aimed not just at careful understanding but at personal transformation.

The ancients loved aphorisms. They believed that although your real aim should be to fill your sails, reason, like a rudder, can steer you in the right direction. Socrates said that wisdom is not like water that can be poured from a jug into a basin. Life's wisdom is manifest in habits and choices, passions and reflection.

So, *42* presents a different approach to the perennial questions of life, happiness and wellbeing – though it is simultaneously an old one. Through analogies and anecdotes, questions and quotes, it applies philosophy to the business of flourishing in life.

THE HAPPY LIFE

1

'Ask yourself whether you are happy and
you cease to be so.'

John Stuart Mill

You would think human beings could agree on some things. Not things like whether a Marmite sandwich is delicious or disgusting or whether bell-bottomed trousers are fashion genius or fashion crime. But things like, for example, what it is to be happy. Of course, this question needs thinking about. But after 250,000 years of existence, 2,500 years of philosophy and 25 unrivalled, rich and revolutionary years of the Internet, it would be reasonable to hope that a consensus had been reached. After all, the smile – the sign of happiness – is universal. And happiness should be a matter of agreement for it is the very reason to live.

However, the history of happiness is a sorry saga. There have always been optimists: the hedonists, who equate happiness with pleasure and seek to maximise the latter. Aristippus of Cyrene was one who made the pursuit of pleasure his life's work. And he was clever. No less a person than Socrates chastised him, pointing out that unrestrained hedonism would make him a slave to his desire and so not happy at all. Aristippus' response was simple and radical. He aimed to indulge in more pleasure than even his desires sought, thereby exerting his authority over them, not they over he.

His approach had one flaw. Excessive pleasure can lead to pain – and even death. Aristippus' admirer, Dionysius I of Syracuse, discovered this when he expired in a delightful but deadly Bacchanalian drinking bout. In response, another of Aristippus' followers, Hegesias, reversed the philosophy: he proposed that it is the avoidance of ot the indulgence of pleasure, that makes for happiness. Since pleasure and pain can be so close, that left only one rational course – the elimination of both: suicide. This conclusion earned Hegesias the label of the 'orator of death'. He must have been persuasive, for his lectures at Alexandria led to a string of student suicides. Yet if the students died content, their *kamikazi* felicity came at a price: the unhappiness of their tutors, who were so distressed that they had Hegesias banned. Ever since, moral authorities have stressed that pleasure is not something that can be pursued willy-nilly. Hedonism hinders the happiness of others.

There is also the question of just what influence someone can have over their happiness. Surely it depends on many things over which one has little or no control; the availability of food and drink, the love of friends and family or the avoidance of crime and calamity. Even today, some of these necessities cannot be taken for granted by at least two-thirds of the world's population. For the remainder, their withdrawal hovers as a possible threat. So, the Cynics said, turn inwards and become self-sufficient, though that cuts out the joy of being with others. Or go with the flow, said the Stoics – which is OK until the flow flows like city traffic.

Christianity further radicalised the problem. One day, Saint Augustine, the towering figure of the church's early theology, passed a beggar on the streets of Milan. He remembered the incident vividly because the man was laughing and joking. A deep sadness welled up inside the saint: he was doing fine in life; that day he had been preparing a speech to be delivered to no less a person than the emperor. He was full of ambition and energy, not just for earthly success but for peace and happiness. And yet, on seeing this smiling man in abject poverty, he turned to his companions in abject misery. This beggar, with nothing, had happiness; he did not. Worse, even though he knew the beggar's happiness was illusory – perhaps brought on by drink or madness – it suggested to him that the path he had adopted was mere contrivance and manoeuvring and could never lead to the simplicity that must be at the heart of felicity. He later realised that happiness was like the sun and thirst. It can neither be viewed unobstructed nor satisfied once and forever.

Why was this? Augustine thought it stemmed from the human desire to be divine. Captured in the story of the Fall, the original sin of Adam and Eve was manifest in the pride of every subsequent individual. The result of not relying on God is the whole history of human evil. Men and women are caught up in a vicious spiral, which flings them about, out of control, under darkening cloudy skies. So serious is the situation that Augustine concluded happiness was not obtainable in this life. Only after death and the death of the selfish self, could anyone reasonably hope for contentment and then only if they had been saved by God. Cast an eye about the world: you do not have to be a Christian to admit there is something powerful in Augustine's pessimism.

Not all Christians agreed. By the Enlightenment, thinkers were in revolt against this theology. The basis for their renewed optimism was what they took to be human progress. Whether through better harvests, growing populations or apparent intellectual gains, 'the sum of well-being is perpetually on the increase,' wrote Jeremy Bentham. The greatest happiness for the greatest number was not just possible but imperative. The eighteenth century was declared the happiest, by eighteenth century optimists. The thought went out that happiness was not just nice to have but a right.

However, this perception of their lot was as flaky as the happiness of the Milanese beggar. Bentham's present-day followers would admit, like his near contemporary Jean-Jacques Rousseau, that progress might not promote happiness but can actually undermine it, in three ways. First, progress rests on factors, such as competitiveness, which cause anxiety. Second, it feeds desires, such as acquisitiveness, which cause dissatisfaction. Third, it creates expectations, such as the desire for happiness, which cause disquiet. 'In the midst of so much philosophy, humanity, politeness and sublime maxims we have merely a deceitful and frivolous exterior: honour without virtue, reason without wisdom and pleasure without happiness,' Rousseau observed.

If little can positively be agreed about happiness, perhaps we should try an alternative strategy for settling the matter. Maybe some markers can be established about what *unhappiness* is. Consider the victim of a merciless disease, dying in writhing agony, denied pain relief by their doctors. Surely that would be an uncontroversial case of unhappiness? No, said Epicurus, who spoke with great authority, having spent his last days in the company of excruciating kidney stones without so much as an aspirin. However, he did not lie on his deathbed longing for the renal failure that would bring merciful release. He rested cheerfully. The terrible is easy to endure, he claimed, because the things that make life happy are so pleasant that they can overwhelm any suffering, as a blanket smothers a fire; he only had to think of the joys of conversing with friends for the pain to pale in comparison. Indeed, because the memory had such power, the happiness they brought was deep and profound. He was nursed by contentment's tranquillity. So, even if Epicurus' peacefulness seems unlikely, unhappiness is out as a candidate for unequivocal agreement. And yet perhaps this in itself tells us something – in fact, three things.

First, thinking about happiness, of itself, does not make you happy. Just as learning does not necessarily make you wise, the study of happiness will not automatically put a smile on your face. Consider a smoker who wants to quit. They decide to be responsible, avoid the places where they habitually light up, fill the times when they usually feel the urge and say a final goodbye to their trusted but destructive cylindrical friends. It is an act of will. 'I just quit,' they want, thereafter, to say. But here comes the catch. The minute they ask themselves how they are going to do it, they see their resolve in perspective. How many times have they tried before? How hard is it going to be? How long life seems without cigarettes! Sartre noticed that this move, from deciding to quit to discussing quitting, is to move from the first person to the third person. In so doing, the individual is no longer just living in the moment, when stopping smoking is relatively easy since it only has to be done in that minute. Rather, they see themselves living on and wonder how on earth they are going to keep it up. This is, perhaps, why people say they can never be a non-smoker but will always be a smoker who is trying to stop. Talking about happiness has the same effect. Being happy is an unselfconscious state; drawing too much attention to it makes it far harder to achieve. Or as John Stuart Mill put it: 'Ask yourself whether you are happy and you cease to be so.'

Second, happiness is not what you might think it is. It seems a natural assumption to equate happiness with pleasure until it becomes clear that pleasures are passing and that happiness depends on things that have nothing to do with pleasure, such as dignity or commitment. Aristotle understood this. He made the point that happiness is not an experience but an activity; more like friendship than pleasure. Or, in other words, happiness is like love: in the same way that you can love your partner without having constant romantic feelings, you can be happy regardless of how you feel in any particular moment.

Happiness might also have much to do with pain. Having children is an action that most people would instinctively believe yields one of life's greatest joys but research shows that children cause as much anxiety as exhilaration. If anything, the balance is tipped against parental pleasure. This is not to say that children are not a great good but rather to realise that children are to do with a much wider understanding of happiness, which includes elements such as giving, hope and love. Again, this happiness stems from a whole way of life. Happiness as pleasure and pleasure alone has at best an occasional, indirect, relationship to these great goods. The ancient Greek philosophers understood this. They incorporated the elusiveness of happiness in their word for it: eudaimonia. 'Eu' means good and 'daimon' means god or spirit. This is not just to say that happiness is something divine but that, like the gods, is something unknown, uncertain, unclear.

These first two paradoxes about happiness add up to a third: happiness is the by-product of a life. At one level, the point is obvious. No one is happy in a vacuum. They are happy because of what they do and who they are; because they love someone or are somewhere. So, to ask, seriously, how to be happy is implicitly to ask a different question: how should I live? This should be the primary concern.

The indirectness of happiness does not stop there, for, if you live a certain way of life solely to be happy, you will not be happy. Consider some of the things self-help books suggest doing to be happy: make friends, take up religion or pursue goals. They suggest these things because the evidence is that religious people with friends and goals are some of the happiest folk alive. However, to turn that observation into a prescription is to put the cart before the horse. Believers are not religious in order to be happy but because they love God. Friends are not sociable in order to be happy but because they like each other. People do not have goals in order to be happy but because they find life meaningful and so pursue goals. Then, indirectly, they are happy.

Where does this leave us? Sextus Empiricus, the sceptic, tells a story that helps. It concerns a painter, Apelles, who was painting a picture of a horse. All was going well until it came to depicting the sweaty froth around the horse's mouth. Apelles tried this technique and that but was always unsatisfied with the result. Finally, in frustration, he picked up the sponge with which he wiped his brushes and flung it at the image. It hit the horse's muzzle, fell off and left a perfect impression of the lather.

Happiness is discovered by chance. But the chance is made by living.

2

'All the advantages of Christianity and alcohol; none of their defects.'

Aldous Huxley on the 'perfect' pleasure-drug, soma, in Brave New World

There once was a creature. It walked on two legs, had a large brain and, over tens of thousands of years of evolution, developed negative and positive mood states. The negative mood states were fear to encourage flight and aggression to encourage it to fight. The positive ones were pleasure and contentment, which rewarded other behaviours advantageous to the creature's survival.

The creature was very successful, so successful that it ceased to be subject to the vagaries of its natural environment and developed technologies that eventually built it a wonderfully conducive world in which to live. No longer did it much need to flee or fight, since it rarely faced mortal dangers. No longer did the creature have to be rewarded for good behaviours, since it was easy to carry out advantageous activities, like eating.

Then things started to go wrong: it was so easy to eat, that an obesity epidemic broke out. This meant the long term mortality rates for the creature started to fall, for the first time in its evolutionary history. Even more bizarrely, things like eating, that before gave only pleasure, became a cause of great unhappiness among the creatures.

Now, some of the creatures were called neuroscientists and some of the neuroscientists not only thought that their work revealed new things about the brains of their fellows but also that they were uncovering the very essence of what it was to be such a being. They developed a new field of enquiry, ontoscience. They were particularly clever; developing pills and procedures that directly influenced the mood states of their fellows by changing the chemical and electrical activity of their large brains. They argued that as a species, they and their fellows had fallen victim to their evolutionary success. They could no more change the desire to overeat than they could start to walk on four legs; they could no more find happiness in their manipulated environment than start to live in the trees. That was just the way it was.

However, the ontoscientists had a solution: they could develop pills and procedures that would allow this tragic creature to be happy and healthy once more. The brain would be directly manipulated to achieve it. One of the ontoscientists had heard of *Brave New World* by Aldous Huxley, though commentators later wondered whether he had actually read it. He named their task, 'Project Soma'.

Some of the other creatures objected to Project Soma. They felt they were more than chemical or electrical machines, to be tuned like an engine. What about the spiritual side of life, they asked? 'Pah!' retorted the ontoscientists: 'Forget that old superstition – it was advantageous on the savannah but it's no use in the city.'

Others worried that while the pills could be useful in extreme cases of unhappiness and unhealthiness, those taking them might live lives free of excessive mood states but also with no real flourishing, creativity or passion. 'Hmm,' thought the ontoscientists: 'But what else are we to do about all our problems? No – we think the pills are best.'

Others argued that if they, as a species, had changed their environment once, then surely they could change it again – perhaps, this time, a little more wisely. Creatures could learn not just to live but to live well. They could step aside from the relentless pursuit of pleasure, which made them so sad and forge habits and an ethos that would lead to a good life. The ontoscientists were suspicious of such talk; it smacked of morality – that deeply unscientific way of thinking, perpetuated by philosophers and theologians. And anyway, ethics was no match for the irresistible forces of evolution.

'Take the pills!' the ontoscientists insisted. And they were well funded and had lots of money with which to spread their message. So the creatures did.

3

'Where ignorance is bliss, 'Tis folly to be wise.'

Thomas Gray

One day, Homer Simpson discovers that he has a crayon in his brain. It nestles between the soft grey folds as snug as a bug in a rug. Any effects the crayon might have are, apparently, negligible. It has been there for many years, ever since, as a child, he attempted to ram an entire box of crayons up his nose; an experiment aborted by a sneeze. Out flew all the crayons, bar this reluctant one. He had not noticed it at all.

Though now he knows about it, he is disconcerted and decides to have the crayon removed. The result is simultaneously amazing and alarming. It is amazing because, after the extraction, he finds himself equipped with new powers of intelligence. His raised appreciation of the world transforms his take on life and, in particular, brings him closer to Lisa, his clever and formerly rather intimidating, daughter. It is alarming because he cannot keep his new perspicuity to himself. What had been hidden from him – poor security at work, the blandness of a movie plot-line – now scream out at him as unbearably bad. In the story Homer blows the whistle on both and is ostracised by everyone around him; they don't want to know about the threat to or the dreariness of life. Everyone, that is, except Lisa, who explains that intelligence has an inverse relationship to happiness: ignorance is bliss. Homer is faced with a choice: live without the crayon or have it put back. Moe, the bartender-cum-surgeon, reinserts it into his brain.

This story, from the 2001 season of the animated television series *The Simpsons*, is retold by Mark Kingwell in *Crayon in the Brain:*

Machining Happiness in the Time of Homer. He uses it to illustrate a conundrum that arises with utilitarian ideas about the pursuit of happiness. Imagine a machine that could make you happy, so perfectly happy that you could not distinguish this induced happiness from the real thing (whatever that might be). Would you plug yourself in? Most people would not, perhaps because they sense this happiness's artificiality would not be authentic or perhaps because they fear a perpetual happiness machine would represent something of a tyranny.

This is what makes Homer's choice so striking. Unplugged from the device that made him happy, albeit a crayon, he could not bear it. But although he admits to Lisa that the reinsertion is cowardly, what is perhaps surprising is that Homer could have found support for his decision in the philosophical tradition - had his temporary intelligence sought it out - for example in Sophocles' story of Oedipus. Oedipus is the man who unwittingly killed his father in an ill-tempered fight by the roadside and unknowingly married his mother, when he was offered her hand as a reward for cracking the riddle of the Sphinx. Oedipus only became aware of these horrors when the prophet Teiresias declared that because of his vile acts, he was the cause of the misfortune that had befallen the city of Thebes. No longer ignorant, Oedipus blinded himself with a pin from the brooch of his wife-mother who, for her part, committed suicide. Part of the pathos of the story stems from the thought that, had his unintended sins remained hidden, Oedipus would have lived a happy life. He could have been saved by a crayon.

The Bible carries a different reflection, in the story of Adam and Eve and the Garden of Eden. They were advised against eating the fruit of the forbidden tree because, should they do so, they would gain knowledge of good and evil. The meaning of the myth has been endlessly debated but one message could be that to have knowledge of good and evil is to have knowledge that only God can bear. Adam and Eve were not gods but human beings. When they ate the fruit, they came into a profound and horrifying awareness of that fact. Henceforth, they were condemned to unhappy lives, infected by toil, shame and murder. Paradise was innocence; ignorance was bliss.

The thought is powerful enough to survive into the post-mythical age. Today, childhood is regarded as the state that should be blissful: there is a moral imperative to preserve its innocence, by withholding knowledge from those deemed too young to bear it. Clearly, children should be protected from things that might harm them but surely not because they are innocent (which Freud and honest parents know they are not).

Homer's guilt for his choice of the crayon over knowledge is a product of the Enlightenment. Many Enlightenment philosophers were aware of the comforts of ignorance but it repelled them. With Kant's clarion call 'Dare to think for yourself!' ringing in their ears, they sought to use the light of reason to chase away the darkness of ignorance, for all that light can be painful. They thought knowledge would ultimately bring happiness. Their conviction was that humanity is too often unhappy not because sadness and suffering is our natural state but because ignorance blocks the way to the achievement of happiness. 'Men are only unhappy because they are ignorant,' opined Baron d'Holbach. A lack of knowledge is manifest in many ills, including injustice, prejudice, false belief and bad practice but – the Enlightenment thinkers argued – as the veil of ignorance was lifted, people would become proportionately more and more happy.

In fact, the straightforward equation of knowledge with happiness was questioned almost immediately. Some asked whose 'knowledge' made who happy. The knowledge of the factory owner, manifest in the doctrines of commerce, allowed them to prosper but only at the expense of the masses. The knowledge of men, manifest in an exclusive social order, might sustain their contentment, while women are not heard and hardly seen. Then there is the question of whether and what knowledge attainable by human beings provides firm foundations for happiness. Is it the truths of religion or those of science that ultimately guarantee it – or a bit of both? What political creed best organises a flourishing society: socialism or capitalism? And socialism or capitalism of what sort? Little wonder that the option of ignorance has retained its appeal.

However, another thought might steel us to living without the crayon. This thought is a distinction that leads to a transformation of Thomas Gray's line. The distinction is the difference between pig-ignorance and wise ignorance. Pig-ignorance is the blindness of the crazed, deluded or wilfully stubborn. Their stupidity may sustain a happiness of sorts but it is a shallow and unstable happiness, often turning into the things the Enlightenment optimists so rightly loathed – injustice, prejudice, false belief and their like. Wise ignorance is a quality of a completely different sort. It is the ignorance of

Socrates, who realised that the key to wisdom is to understand the limits of what you know. This insight came to him after he received a startling message from the Delphic Oracle, which had ventured that no one was wiser than he: something Socrates knew could not be right, since he was highly aware of what little he knew. So, he set out to prove the Oracle wrong, by speaking to all the wise people of Athens. He was disappointed. Politicians, he realised, believe their own hype. Poets, he saw, are brilliant with words but mistake that brilliance for wisdom. Professionals, he concluded, might be experts in their field but are wrong if they take that professionalism to mean they are experts in life as a whole. Then he understood. No one was wiser than he, because no one understood the depth of their ignorance as fully as he did. We are all ignorant but the smart thing is to become wise of the fact.

This wise ignorance brought Socrates a profound sense of contentment. When he was condemned to death by the Athenian state he did not flee the city, as he easily could have done. He stayed, comforted his followers, drank the hemlock and died.

In short, pig-ignorance is a paltry bliss and wise ignorance supreme; a truth that appears in other traditions. Thomas Aquinas believed that happiness was something that could only completely be found in heaven. However, the very fact that human beings can understand that, by appreciating the flaws of their 'in between' condition, allows them a happiness-of-becoming on earth. This also suggests that happiness is not just a matter of understanding – something that is always incomplete for mortals; it is also a matter of will, a will that always seeks more. Do not people often desire things before they understand them, like fame or fortune? And that desire brings with it a share in the thing sought, even if only in the voyeurism of glossy magazines or the thrill of lottery tickets. How much more, then, will wise desires - like the desire for divine contentment - bring a deeper happiness. 'Love enters where knowledge is left outside,' Thomas writes – and that makes for happiness here and now.

The Daoist teacher, Zhuangzi, contributed another take on the wise ignorance that is happiness, when he recalled a dream. One day, around sunset, he dozed off and imagined that he had become a butterfly. He flapped his wings and, yes, he flew! Such was the glory of the experience that he completely forgot he was Zhuangzi. After a little while, however, it occurred to him that the proud butterfly was really Zhuangzi dreaming he was a butterfly. Or, dreaming on, was it that he was a butterfly imagining that it was Zhuangzi? Maybe Zhuangzi was the butterfly and maybe the butterfly was Zhuangzi?

Zhuangzi awoke and though he knew again that he was a philosopher, his visionary merging of realities suggested to him that his knowledge of himself was limited, possibly completely delusory. What he had learnt - or rather unlearnt – was what he had taken himself to be. 'Real knowledge is to know the extent of one's ignorance,' was Confucius' summary of the insight. Zhuangzi had never been so happy.

Wise ignorance is not just a philosophical or religious sentiment. It also drives science, if science is a quest for the unknown. Many things of a certain sort are discovered by its methods and sometimes put to good use as technology. But good science itself regards discovery as just another horizon, a place from which to peer further, all the more intelligently. This is its joy, not wrapping up but continuously unwrapping.

So be rid of the crayons and discover a deeper, happier ignorance! 'One of the greatest joys known to man is to take such a flight into ignorance in search of knowledge,' concluded the essayist, Robert Lynd. 'The great pleasure of ignorance is, after all, the pleasure of asking questions. The man who has lost this pleasure or exchanged it for the pleasure of dogma, which is the pleasure of answering, is already beginning to stiffen.'

4

'Things can only get better.'

Political slogan

'Workers of the world, unite!'

The famous revolutionary slogan of Marx and Engel's *Communist Manifesto* was eventually trounced by 'Better dead than red'. That was originally a piece of Nazi propaganda, launched against the Russian enemy but it was adopted by post-war American politicians, the side that eventually won the Cold War.

Powerful political slogans like these straddle two worlds, the world of ideology and the world of the individual. They aim to pull the two together, drawing people into the orbit of their sentiment, so that they feel the slogan is their own. This is why the Australian Prime Minister, John Howard's, 2001 election slogan 'We decide who comes here', was so devastatingly effective. It is why one proposed anti-Hillary Clinton slogan for the 2008 election: 'Read my lips – no more interns', while witty, packs little political punch; it is a joke, not a unifying vision of national and individual life.

'Things can only get better' was the default slogan of the British Labour Party's landslide victory of 1997. On first reading it sounds a bit bland, the kind of comforting sentiment a grandmother might offer, rounded off with a kindly 'dear'. This, in a way, was its genius, for while the 'better' ostensibly referred to better politicians, better finances and better services, it also carried the hint that 'life' would also be better under New Labour. Labour's spin doctors alluded as closely as they dared to a promise that they knew people would laugh at if it were explicit – a politician's promise of happiness. But would they laugh? Since 1997, happiness has risen in the political agenda. In the UK, over 80 per cent of people say the government should focus on making people happier, not wealthier and an advisor to the former British Prime Minister, Tony Blair, believed that by 2020 governments will be measured by how happy they make their citizens.

Often referred to as the politics of well-being, the appeal of happiness arises from an observation. Affluent Western citizens have become richer in the last hundred years and yet, some time after the Second World War, they stopped becoming happier. Since Aristotle, most theorists have supposed that the aim of politics is the collective good, so, if the good that people aspire to is happiness, perhaps politicians should re-think their roles. It's not the economy, stupid, it's felicity!

Two countries are held up as paradigms of such a possibility: Bhutan and Denmark. In the former, remote Himalayan kingdom, the measure of politics is not Gross Domestic Product but Gross National Happiness. Denmark, on the other hand, recently came top of the list in a worldwide survey of subjective well-being. What, other than small populations and cold winters, these two countries have that others don't is not clear. Bhutan is semi-feudal, suggesting that happiness is a product of knowing your place in society. The academic who spotted Denmark's bliss puts it down to an excellent health service. There is not much encouragement for politicians in either case: feudalism is unsellable and the reform of health services is notoriously prone to failure.

What is sometimes referred to as the 'science of happiness' gives politicians more hope. Also called positive psychology, it asks why, to quote Freud, psychology not only might replace neurotic unhappiness with normal unhappiness but also turn normal unhappiness into positive happiness. Positive psychology studies the various factors that could contribute to this transformation. Martin Seligman, the movement's founder, is modest about what it can attain – a 10 to 15 per cent rise in happiness in the average person – which is perhaps why his insights often sound like so much motherhood and apple-pie: 'work less', 'maintain the family', 'keep fit', 'find meaning'. Living in a 'wealthy democracy' not an 'impoverished dictatorship' takes first place on Seligman's list of external effects that can raise your happiness levels. And now a cure for cancer, professor!

Seligman is right, inasmuch as external factors do play a crucial role in people's happiness and politics can shape these external factors. Even the Stoics, who toyed with the idea that someone could be happy on the rack, concurred. They just thought that you had to learn to ignore things around you. So how might the politics of well-being profitably proceed? There are three thorny problems to be addressed; thorny because they sit very uneasily alongside the traditional politics of economic growth; indeed, they go a long way to explaining why that approach has failed us.

The first might be referred to as consumer melancholy syndrome – CMS for short. Though not under that name, it was well articulated by Rousseau, as a result of the identification of happiness with pleasure. Three unintended consequences of this equivalence cause CMS. First, pleasures only satisfy desires; they do not fulfil them – leaving people sated but sad. Second, people become slaves to these desires and so suffer the unhappiness of that enslavement. Third, this slavish unhappiness is exacerbated, because people find they are not happy even though they think happiness should be their right. 'Happiness leaves us or we leave it,' Rousseau despaired.

The second problem was captured by the philosopher Bernard Williams, in a thought experiment. Imagine, he said, a world in which people could be shot instead of receiving parking tickets. Overnight, the parking problem would be solved. A few people might die but in the cost-benefit analysis – the methodology at the heart of modern economics – those deaths could be excused, because of the greater happiness that would be brought to millions. Any sane person would recoil at such a policy and a more sophisticated economist could demonstrate that another cost-benefit analysis shows why: millions of people would be made unhappy as a result of the capital threat hanging over them. However, Williams argued that it is not the calculation that shows the policy to be wrong. It is wrong because such calculations are deployed at all. No matter how sophisticated, calculations cannot help but treat people as pawns. They ignore the fact that people are people and should be nurtured for their own sake. In other words, it is the lack of human sympathy in the decision-making of economists that alienates people and has much to do with modern unhappiness.

The third challenge to the politics of well-being can be associated with Adam Smith. In his *The Theory of Moral Sentiments* he worried about the effects on the way people lived of the commercial society he saw emerging around him. He realised that capitalism was replacing the ancient goal of politics – happiness – with something else, which he identified as social cooperation. Social cooperation seemed a mundane thing to aspire to, he thought, for all that it has the merit of steering human beings away from wars and requires people to act justly, beneficently and prudently – the very virtues of democracy. But what of the higher goal of happiness?

There might be one way in which social cooperation increases happiness: 'A great part, perhaps the greatest part, of human happiness and misery arises from the view of our past conduct and from the degree of approbation or disapprobation which we feel from the consideration of it,' Smith thought. Social cooperation encourages people to conduct themselves admirably and therefore in praiseworthy ways – 'a job well done', 'I was glad to help' – from which they will gain a sense of satisfaction and, from that, happiness. This might well be so, in an ideal world. However, praiseworthiness does not always receive the praise it deserves. Moreover, at work, say, that which is praised may have little to do with praiseworthiness. For in a world defined by commerce and competition, delivery merits the attention; at work, people are remunerated for what they do, not who they are; qualities that might make someone praiseworthy are likely simply to be ignored or take second place. Hence the problem of alienation at work: it can make you very unhappy.

The compulsions of consumerism, the calculatedness of cost-benefit analysis and the ambivalent virtues of social cooperation. These are the challenges the politics of well-being must face. Little wonder politicians hold off any direct promise of happiness. Little wonder we wouldn't believe them if they didn't.

5

'Man's unhappiness springs from one thing alone, his incapacity to stay quietly in one room.'

Blaise Pascal

Imagine an artist who makes Arabesque mosaics from tiny pieces of paper. For weeks, she works alone in her studio. With nothing more than sharp scissors, multi-coloured scrolls, scraps and obsession, she snips and cuts, cuts and collates. Then, in the creative part of her work, she glues each piece in place. To say it is painstaking is like saying snails are slow.

The result is exquisite. The colour, precision, unity and complexity of the geometric forms are as wonderfully constructed as the tesserae of a Moorish floor or the knots of a Persian carpet. The brilliance of her art is that the infinite nature of the divine, the reason for the Islamic love of intricate, repeated patterns, is represented in the very fabric of her work and in the infinite care of her labour. The madness of making the mosaics from paper cuttings captures something utterly remarkable.

But stop! I must avoid rationalising what she does, for it rationalises it away. To talk of the work aesthetically or intellectually puts a distance between us and the art's power to disturb. And to lose sight of its madness, her patient obsession, is to make it comfortable. It is easy to enjoy it as a thing of beauty or a subject for conjecture but it is frightening to think of her spending all that time cutting and collating. Her crazy commitment is its challenge. Think of the monotony. Think of the life without diversion. Think of the capacity to sit attentively in a studio for hour after hour, day after day. The art has power because it questions an opposite conception of life based on endless novelty and choice.

Imagine visiting her studio. It probably has plain white walls and unforgiving fluorescent lighting; harsh but vital for the examination of myriad fragments of paper. A fidget would soon find themselves playing with scraps. A demonstrative person would perhaps start to pace the room. Someone who was easily embarrassed would soon be searching for polite ways of making their exit. An intellectual would stave off rising panic with 'engaging' questions – though the effect would be to keep the work at a distance. It captivates her but, if the visitor were honest, it quickly bores or frightens them.

What the artist has is an excellence, an activity that she executes supremely well and that occupies her above all things. Like a magnetic pole drawing a compass, the work orients her whole life. As thoroughly as a neurotic, though positive because productive, it is embedded in her like a habit. It is coterminous with her character. She obeys it.

This is why the work is frightening. The life of the artist, which might be thought of as free and expressive, is constrained and – to the visitor – oppressive. The thought of it prompts a round of questions about life. Is the life of novelty and choices – the life of the visitor-consumer – antithetical to the life of excellence, the life of the artist? If the patient regard of the artist is a kind of love, where is love in the need for distraction? Is obedience needed to find bliss? If so, why, to what and how?

The 'desert fathers' of the early Christian church captured something of these conundrums in one of the seven deadly sins, which they referred to as *acedia*. *Acedia* can be roughly translated as 'boredom'. In his gripping book, *A Philosophy of Boredom*, Lars Svendsen explains why boredom was thought so deadly:

> Evagrius Ponticus (c. 345–399) conceives acedia as being demonic. The midday demon (daemon meridianus) is the most cunning of all demons, attacking the monk in the middle of the day, in broad daylight, causing the sun to seem to be standing utterly still in the sky. Things intrude on this state but appear to be completely de-animated. The demon causes him to detest the place where he finds himself – and even life itself.

In other words, to detest life is to detest God, hence the mortal peril of boredom.

Pascal modernised the concept, by linking boredom with diversions, the many things people do to avoid ennui. So great is people's fear of unhappiness, he notes, that they will flock to the slightest thing if it promises distraction – 'like tapping a billiard ball with a cue,' he jokes at the snooker fan's expense.

The problem with diversions is that they obey a diminishing law of returns. Over time, they become boring, because they do not engage the individual; they only distract them. As diversions, they have nothing excellent about them. The situation can rapidly deteriorate: in Chuck Palahiuk's novel *Fight Club*, the dull distractions of the consumer lifestyle, manifest in the narrator's insomnia, leads him to the eponymous Fight Club, an underground meeting of men who engage in a therapy of bloody, bare-knuckle fighting. Violence is not happiness but it is a perverse kind of excellence, which staves off boredom.

In J.G. Ballard's novel *Super-Cannes*, boredom is portrayed not as a critique of a consumer lifestyle but as a product of a life in business. Ballard's protagonist is offered an apparently perfect job in a fictitious business park, Eden-Olympia, in the gorgeous setting of the hills above Cannes. However, he notices that an epidemic of insomnia has invaded corporate paradise. As the plot unfurls, the companies operating in Eden-Olympia become worried about it too – because it is detrimentally affecting their employees' productivity. They fabricate a night life of crime, prostitution and drugs for their staff, in the hope that these diversions will take away their boredom and re-ignite their creativity.

If violence or alarm were not distracting enough, then perhaps shock could do the trick. Arguably, this is the diversion that the art establishment has tried in the 'shock of the new' and then the 'shock of the old'. The assumption is that art is in danger of becoming stuck in a soporific rut. Like a bolt of lightning (and lasting as long) what is deemed necessary for art to be art is for it to crack conceptions with 'interventions' conceived by celebrity artists. Only they can have the power to drag art and its public out of the mire. The celebrity artists do not need to make the art and anyway, they don't have the time. They too need distracting, at fabulous openings and extravagant parties.

A doctrine of choice proliferation is damaging because it feeds the culture of diversion. It peddles excitement as excellence, greener grass as happiness. Think of the bread aisles in a supermarket: brown bread, white bread, granary bread, rye bread, thick sliced, thin sliced, bruschetta, chollah, ciabatta, focaccia, fresh garlic, gluten-free, nan organic, pitta. Clearly, a degree of choice is good. Some people need gluten-free. But why is the humble baguette – which splits to release its fresh, chalky scents – so lovely? Its simplicity outshines the choice of the supermarket. It is excellent. It is enough. The supermarket range becomes so much noise and distraction.

How can we understand the hidden life achieved by the snipping and cutting, cutting and pasting of the non-celebrity artist? Imagine an isosceles triangle, its short side on the horizontal and its two, equally long sides rising, like a pyramid, above it. One of the lower corners represents ennui, the other excitement. The third, at the peak of the pyramid, is excellence. It is easy to spend life on the horizontal, oscillating between the extremes of ennui and excitement. The trick is to turn your eyes upwards, to develop a way of life that reaches higher, towards excellence. Ennui and excitement will persist, for a time and in a way are fine. But instead of swinging helplessly between them, you might rise. To be excellent is to transcend them both.

6

'The thinker philosophises as the lover does.'

William James

Voltaire wrote a story about a good Brahmin. The Brahmin spent forty years pondering big questions and then suddenly, one day, came to a halt. He declared that he wished he had never been born. 'I have been studying these forty years and I find that it has been so much time lost,' he cried. Soon after, he fell into conversation with his neighbour, an old woman. Caught up in his crisis, 'I asked her if she had ever been unhappy for not understanding how her soul was made?' The old woman did not even comprehend the Brahmin's question, let alone answer it.

You might think this would double his agony but it does not. Her incomprehension is his breakthrough. He realises that he does not desire the happiness of a 'contented automaton'. Connection, which the old woman has, is the key to his happiness. He had not been mistaken to love big questions. His mistake had been to prefer prosaic answers to passionate ones.

Voltaire wrote in an age in which philosophy sought the more and more abstract. In the attempt to arrive at arguments that were universal and true, its utterances were becoming detached, its gaze imperious. Many contemporary philosophers would say that their discipline's abstraction from their or anyone's biography is one of its greatest achievements and makes the quest for what is objectively true possible. Like a scientist, they think of their task as being above the fray of living. They do not see that imagining they can – and should –

keep their hands clean of the messy business of life's pageant means they become abstract and lose touch.

This would have bemused the ancient Greek philosophers. It is not that they did not do abstract: it is that they didn't do it for its own sake. For them, the thinker did not philosophise as the lover did. The philosopher and the lover do the same thing.

Plutarch describes these heady days, focusing on the ecstasy of what was then called natural philosophy:

> No man yet, on having intercourse with the woman he loves, has been so happy that he went out and sacrificed an ox; nor has anyone ever prayed to die on the spot if he could only have his fill of royal meat or cakes. But Eudoxus prayed to be consumed in flames like Phaethon if he could only stand next to the sun and ascertain the shape, size and composition of the planets; and when Pythagoras discovered his theorem he sacrificed an ox, as Apollodorus records.

Plato explores the synthesis in another way. In his dialogue, *Phaedrus*, he describes how human love can be transfigured, to become a love of philosophy powered by friendship. He describes this process with a case study that mixes philosophy and biography, beginning with Socrates bumping into his friend Phaedrus. They lie down by the river and talk together about life and love. Conversing on these matters could not be easier or more natural to them on that day, since they are both in love: Socrates with Isocrates; Phaedrus with Lysias. This charting of the state of their relationships – the thing that lovers love to do – provides the raw material, as it were, for philosophical reflection. Plato toys with the question of whether the best kind of love is driven by erotic or philosophical desire. He concludes that, at best, the two coincide.

The lover, at first, is simply propelled viscerally towards their beloved. Part of that love is animal: it drives the lover, like a chariot pulled by a wild horse. But part of it is more human, wishing goodwill on the beloved. With luck, the lover catches the beloved's eye, who is disposed to respond positively: it is always lovely to be lovable.

Should they click, after talking together, something new begins to emerge in their relationship. Both are amazed by the realisation that this nascent friendship looks like it is worth more than relationships they have experienced before. Like an echo that amplifies in a cavern, their love bounces between them and grows. Like a spiritual drink, it fills them body and soul. Disreputable poets have rhymed the word 'love' with 'shove', Plato recalls. The rhyme should be between 'love' and 'above', such are the heights the two can now reach.

Some lovers are false to one another: they are spiteful, hostile or make a pretence of passion. But for true lovers, the mutuality of their aspirations and character works magic: it fosters a sense of awe. They are amazed to be alive. Their full-blooded love opens up a passion, not just for each other but for life itself, for philosophy. True lovers want to know what love is; it discloses new insights; it lives with greater intensity; it precipitates big questions. Some of this is pure madness but not all madness is delusory: it has an energy that breaks through the forces that would otherwise hold people back.

This is the power of love. It can triumph over the nervous calculations that people make in relationships; it can connect the intellect to a kind of knowledge that is beyond the purely abstract, objective and rational. This has been wisely called 'love's knowledge'. It is subjective; it is true because it is true for me.

Such love might be called an erotic friendship, driven not so much by a desire for each other – something that inevitably cools with time – but by a thirst for that which is beyond both and must be shared. Elsewhere, Plato associates this with the creative urge to have children or to cultivate ideas. Such friendship lies at the heart of what he takes philosophy to be. Two philosophers, Giles Deleuze and Félix Guattari, have gone so far as to suggest that to call Plato's philosophy 'philosophy' is a misnomer. It should really be called erosophy.

THE EVERYDAY LIFE

7

'As for sex, it is the rubbing together of pieces of gut, followed by the spasmodic secretion of a little bit of slime.'

Marcus Aurelius

In 2005, Professor Gert Holstege, using a PET scanner, did what thousands of neuroscientists are now doing all around the world. He recorded the brain activity of some women and men. The difference was he did it not while they were making decisions or carrying out tests but while they were having an orgasm.

In an ideal world, he would have liked to have seen what was going on inside his subjects' heads during normal sexual intercourse. That was simply not possible, because PET scanning requires people to lie still. Instead, lying still, his game guinea-pigs were 'manually stimulated' to climax (by right-handed 'partners', to accommodate the shape of the scanner.) Their heads were restrained and they had to hold the rest of their bodies immobile, in case extraneous neurone firings swamped the brain activity associated with the orgasm. And as if that were not bizarre enough, the couples had to be able to 'do it' in the clinical environment of the laboratory. Unsurprisingly, about half the people that Professor Holstege recruited found they could not 'perform' under such un-conducive conditions. The less inhibited experimented with various states of undress. Draughts in the scanning room led to the consensus that whatever else they took off, socks were kept on, to avoid getting 'cold feet'.

Then there was the business of actually capturing the action. The problem was that, as everyone knows, the female orgasm is a long-lived, endlessly repeatable experience, unlike the male orgasm, which is over in just a few short seconds. A PET scan ideally requires the activity being observed to last for two minutes and, if possible, to be repeated several times, to allow the images to be collated. *Ipso facto*, male climaxes are scarcely more than a sigh, at least as far as the scanner is concerned.

There was also the question of just what was being recorded. In addition to the mechanical abnormality of the acts themselves, science does not have a good definition of what was supposedly being studied; orgasm. It cannot just be activity in the genital area, like ejaculation, because some men can ejaculate without orgasm. Neither can it be only viscero-somatic, a climax of racing hearts, rising blood pressure, flushing skins and uncontrollable muscular spasms, because these things come and go during sex. Perhaps sex is cerebral; an electrical storm of joy, pleasure, ecstasy and emotion? That somehow seems more resonant with our virtual age though, strictly speaking, it won't do either: research on people with severe spinal injuries has shown that they can climax without any sense of euphoria. However, for Professor Holstege that definition would have to do.

Needless to say, when his results were announced, the newspapers could not resist the story. *The Times* of London put it and pictures of the orgasming brains, on page three, in celebration of the tabloid tradition: 'For women, pleasure is (nearly) all in the mind', ran the headline, followed by the results of the research: male brains concentrate on physical stimulation; women need to feel relaxed: men feel more passion at the peak of orgasm; women enter a trance-like state.

Professor Holstege was flirting with the punishment of Tiresias. The Homeric prophet had been both a man and a woman. Having experienced sex as both, Zeus asked him to settle an argument between himself and his wife, Hera: who experienced greater pleasure during copulation, men or women? Tiresias decided in favour of women, saying it was ten times better. You might have thought Hera would be pleased: she was not. She took offence, feeling her love-making skills had been insulted. She blinded the transsexual prophet.

Professor Holstege has not gone blind, as far as I know. In some ways it's different, in some ways it's the same, he wisely suggested. On the other hand, his results confirmed that women are skilled enough to fake an orgasm, though not skilled enough to fool the scanner.

It has been said that while the modern person asks themself, '*Should* I have sex?', the ancient person would have asked himself

[sic], '*How* should I have sex?' The difference carried by the addition of that small word is the difference between an approach to sex coloured by anxieties about its goodness and an approach to sex coloured by anxieties about its benefits.

Roughly, the story goes that in ancient Athens, the citizens discussed 'the things of Aphrodite' under the assumption that everything was possible, because sex was naturally good, but not everything was advisable. One could engage in heterosexual, homosexual, marital and extra-marital sex: the question was the use to which such pleasures might be put and with what degree of indulgence. Under Christianity, the fundamental assumptions changed. Not everything was possible, because the goodness of sex had become problematic. Many sexual activities were simply prohibited. At the time of Pericles, the ithyphallic member would have been seen on every street corner – on statues of Hermes, in images of Bacchus, on murals and doorbells. But after the first century CE, an erection became 'the image of man in revolt against God,' as Michel Foucault put it.

Consider the great sex scene in Plato's dialogue, the *Symposium*. It features Socrates and Alcibiades, his student, who was as gorgeous as James Dean and as deserving of the title given to the film that made Dean a star. Alcibiades is infatuated and has wooed Socrates into his bed. At last, he thinks, I have the old tease in a place where my erotic powers are irresistible. He was wrong. Though they lay wrapped in the same cloak all night, Socrates declined his advances. He loved Alcibiades but wanted to share the gold of intellectual passion with him, not the bronze of his tumescent sexuality.

Note that Socrates does not say that it would wrong for them to make love – as the Christian moralist might because of the homosexual element or as the secular ethicist might because of their pedagogical relationship. Rather, he says that it would not be the *best* thing for them to do. They could but to do so would be to confuse the yearnings of the body with the yearnings of the soul and, by indulging the former, risk dampening the latter. This, incidentally, is the original meaning of a Platonic relationship: not one free of physical desire but one in which that desire is well-directed. Thus the question, not should I have sex but *how* should I have sex?

This attitude towards sex had a paradoxical outcome. Far from being a free-for-all, as if ancient life were one long toga-party, it led to intricate debates about sex: hence the 'how'. Moreover, it led, on occasion, to the celebration of ideals that could compete with the toughest modern-day Puritanism. Pausanias, another character in Plato's *Symposium*, compared the customs of various Greek cities regarding love. He approved most of those places, like Athens, where the customs were the most complex. His reason was that sophisticated customs, which weighed issues from appropriate age to appropriate conduct, winnowed the chaff of vulgar acts from the wheat of higher love. The highest, according to Pausanius, was demonstrated in wanting to share everything with your lover for the rest of your life.

Pausanias was wholly unlike any puritan. He disapproved most of those cities that imposed moral codes, of which the worst was outright proscription. These cities banned certain practices not because sex was thought to be wrong but because it was thought to be too complex an issue to negotiate without the heavy hand of the law as a guide. The price for such clarity, Pausanius argued, was that love itself was stymied. 'How' could not be asked: sex was treated simply as a matter of obeying moral rules.

An obvious objection to this history of attitudes towards sex would be to attack the first assumption made; that the modern person even asks themselves the lesser question, 'Should I have sex?' Surely the objection would be that since the invention of the Pill and the liberation of men and women from so-called Victorian values, this is the last question on people's minds. Rather, both questions have been rejected and replaced by an imperative: 'Have Sex!' No doubt, on very many occasions, this is true and arguably, if on not quite so many occasions, it has led to jolly nice sex. However, notice that the little word 'how' is now not only missing but its place has been lost. With that go even the rules.

The philosopher Michel Foucault, who spotted the difference between ancient Greek and Christian attitudes, also noticed this most recent change – not least because, as a gay man, he gained from it: the permissiveness of the 'have sex' generation has made for much greater openness when it comes to exploring what once were illicit acts. However, he did not miss what was lost with the obliteration of the 'how'. He worried about it. Do we not still live in an age in which human sexuality is mostly about bodies and ideally, beautifully equipped bodies, he asked? Is not modern sex typically a question of performance and ideally, exceptional and enhanced performance?

Many would agree with these worries when it comes to, for example, the burgeoning porn industry but such obvious cases were not primarily what Foucault had in his sights. Rather, he wondered whether the loss of the 'how' was the outcome of what he termed a *scientia sexualis*, a science of sex that has perhaps undermined the ancient *ars erotica* even more profoundly than the first Christians.

This brings us back to Professor Holstege's experiments. Along with others like it, this alternative 'sex industry' objectifies lovemaking as profoundly as does any chick flick. It is no doubt aimed at some greater good, such as a cure for impotence or the increase of human knowledge. The trouble is what the study involves and the way it is received. By its very nature, the *scientia sexualis* removes sex from its interpersonal context – the sphere in which the question 'how should I have sex?' is asked – and places it in a sphere in which even the 'should I ...' question is discarded. It turns sex from being a moral question, whether asked in the ancient or Christian mode, to a biological question – a matter of measurement and functions, of performance and physiology. The double worry is that science has such huge status in contemporary society that its results, plastered across the newspapers, come to be mistaken for the meaning of sex.

This is what makes Marcus Aurelius' bleak thought so prescient: is the contemporary, scientific understanding of sex anything more than 'the rubbing together of pieces of gut, followed by the spasmodic secretion of a little bit of slime'?

8

'Photography is truth. Cinema is truth at twenty-four times per second.'

Jean-Luc Godard

Consider a moment from Alfred Hitchcock's classic, *Saboteur*. Frank Fry, the saboteur, is in a taxi, looking out of the window. The next shot cuts to an ocean liner, the *SS Alaska*, capsizing by a pier. You may not have seen the film but you already know what has happened: the capsized ship is Fry's handiwork.

We automatically make the connection, because we know the language of the cinema. The actor who played Fry never saw the ship; it was several thousand miles away in New York. Neither was he ever in a taxi driving down a street; the journey was faked in a studio. But the viewer easily makes the connections, turning the cuts into a coherent whole with an innate fluency that is repeated time and again whenever they watch a film.

Why is the cinematic language so readily understandable? Why don't we see a series of disconnected fragments – a taxi, a striking man, a ship? The answer is simple: because we don't want to. We yearn for a continuous narrative; we crave relationships and connections in the darkened hall of the cinema. So powerful is this desire that it supports a multi-billion dollar industry.

'Blockbusters' could be defined as those films that most profoundly satisfy this desire. Think of *The Lord of the Rings* trilogy or the *Matrix* movies. They are not only brilliantly produced and edited but also tell stories of mythical reconnection, hope winning over despair and good over evil; stories that precisely resonate with the pleasure of cinematic connection. The world is not a series of fragments: it makes sense! The medium merges with the message.

A similar thing could be said about romantic movies. Their narrative is of the connection found in love: little wonder that the silver screen makes us weep like no other art form. Mel Gibson's *The Passion of The Christ* (a 'religious horror movie', as the church-going film critic Mark Kermode has called it) works because its horror element shocks the viewer out of their ordinary experience in a way that parallels the religious experience evoked by ecstatic devotion in the suffering of the saints.

To someone with a religious frame of reference, the irresistible experience that comes about when a film fires an individual's imagination, be it at the level of myth, romance or horror, is entirely understandable. Why do we love cinema? The final answer is not because it is entertaining but because, to echo Saint Augustine, our hearts are restless. We long for life to make sense. We love it when we find meaning. Cinema offers such a catharsis. As the titles roll, we can find an almost transcendent calm.

9

'The innocent sleep.'

Macbeth

I've just had a bad night's sleep. Only four hours up to 3.15 am. Then, between six and eight, a couple of hours drifting in and out of consciousness. The after-effects have persisted during the morning, leaving a mental fog in the soggy gullies of my mind that the clarity of the day can't quite reach.

Such a night serves to remind me of one of the many paradoxes of sleep. For every other bodily pleasure – such as sex, seeing or eating – the more intense the experience the more satisfaction it brings. Sleep is the opposite: less perception is greater pleasure. That is why insomnia is such a curse.

The hours of unreality have a particular character, elucidated by Freud in *The Interpretation of Dreams*, where he tells the story of a father whose son has died. While asleep one night, he dreams that his son is standing by his bed mouthing haunting words: 'Father, can't you see that I'm burning?' The father awakes. He smells real burning. Horrified, he realises that a candle has fallen on the shroud covering his son's corpse and it is on fire.

Freud thought that the father smelt the burning while asleep and incorporated it into a dream in order to stay asleep. He only woke up when his dreaming could no longer deny the reality of the actual flames. If he is right, dreaming exists to keep us asleep. Even if that means nightmares, their horror is better than whatever reality waits to haunt us should we wake. It also explains why the hours of insomnia are filled with concerns. The insomniac should be dreaming these worries away, not fretting about them through the night. It is not so much that the innocent sleep, as that even dreams cannot keep the insomniac from their anxieties.

10

'They say travel broadens the mind; but
you must have the mind.'

G. K. Chesterton

To the traveller, fewer countries offer greater delight than one darkened and derided in contemporary politics: Syria. There is Apamea, a Roman city that overlooks the broad plain of the Orontes valley. Like the more famous Palmrya, located in the desert halfway to the Euphrates, Apamea is remarkably preserved. The colonnade of its *cardo maximus* (main street) rises out of the cultivated fields that cover most of the site, well over a mile long, taking your eye to infinity in a dazzle of white marble. The façades of the shops that once lined the street are also intact (or reconstructed). A walk along the *cardo* as the sunlight softened in the cool of the day must have been an urban pleasure rarely exceeded either then or since.

Or, consider the crusader castle of Saône, also known as Qalaat Saladin. Krak de Chevalier might steal a march in terms of glory but Saône wins in beauty. It is poised on a luscious green ridge that rises out of a deep gorge. The view west, as the sun sets over the golden surface of the Mediterranean, makes the valley leading down to the coast seem like a pathway to heaven. No wonder the romantic crusaders built a fortress here, despite, as T. E. Lawrence pointed out, its site fatally compromising its military strength: Saladin took the place in just a couple of days. Typically for one of Syria's tourist sites, it was more or less deserted for my visit to its groined and cradled vaults. A particularly delightful find was a water cistern on the north wall, a tall arched room with a continuous roof 32 metres long, giving it 15 seconds of reverberation. In such an acoustic, a clever singer could perform a solo four part harmony.

But an even more a remote spot had caught my eye in a travel book: Nebi Uri, on Syria's border with Turkey. The only practical way to reach it is to hire a taxi for the day which, although at around $100 was by far the most expensive way to travel, meant that my party could take in a couple of other sites en route. We were staying in the refitted Baron Hotel in Aleppo, whose guests have included T. E. Lawrence and Agatha Christie: neither known for taking the easy path. In similar spirit, we decided to go it alone rather than fix the trip via the hotel's manager Walid. 'There is nothing I cannot do for you, Mr Mark,' he told me several times.

Declining his offer did pose a problem. Not only is Nebi Uri hard to pronounce in Arabic, (being full of vowels) but it is also known by several other names. We thought we might overcome this nominal issue by pointing to Cyrrhus on the map. This settlement, which flourished in the second century, is close to Nebi Uri and a more routine tourist sight, due to possessing two Roman hump-backed bridges that carry traffic to this day. However, Syrians seem to place little trust in maps, particularly when it comes to spots on the Turkish border; bloody territorial disputes have turned maps into potentially subversive documents. Although taxi-drivers obligingly looked at our map while we tried to explain the destination and seal a deal, no sooner had we finished than they would turn to any passer-by willing to express an opinion and discuss where this elusive place might be. We made little progress.

The solution came via a contact, Serop Megerditchian, the pastor at the Armenian Evangelical Emmanuel Church, who spoke English. In true Middle Eastern style, he was as generous as Abraham serving the angels. Location sorted, a member of his church community, a taxi driver by the name of George Nasser, was telephoned and appeared a few short minutes later. We were due to depart the next morning.

George met us at the Baron and before leaving the city we went to his family's apartment to pick up his daughter Manya, who wanted to come along and practise her English. She became the most valuable member of our party. For one thing, it turned out that George had never before left Aleppo: he crossed himself three times as we traversed its boundary. Perhaps Manya, as the first generation to have no direct memories of the pain, did not feel the fear that her father seemed to when the Turkish border was in prospect. 'My great-grandfather and his family were forced to march from Turkey,' she told us. 'My great-grandmother died on the way and my great-uncle was shot. I will teach my children the story and take them to Deir ez Zor' (the eastern town on the Euphrates where a cathedral has been erected to commemorate the two million who died).

We stopped off first at Mushabbak which, as Howard Butler said, in his *Early Churches in Syria, fourth to seventh centuries*, is one of the most perfectly preserved of all the many Byzantine basilicas in the region. A hundred years ago, he noted that replacing the fallen stones of the gables and the restoration of its wooden roofs was all that was required to make it a practical house of worship. Little had changed in the century since. Next came the remains of the neo-Hittite temple of Ain Dara, which has sat proudly on a low plateau in the valley of the Afrin river since the start of the first millennium BCE. The crumbled walls of the temple still rise a couple of feet above the ground, enough to show a frieze of lions and sphinxes that guard the confines of the Holy of Holies. The steps of the main entrance are marked by massive footprints, one metre long, signifying the godly presence. They are still remarkably effective, if today looking more extra-terrestrial than divine. Most surprising of all are the 'Celtic' designs that adorn what remains of the porticoes. This art existed in Syria for 1500 years before being brought, by the Frisians or Angles, to Britain.

On our journey the roads were becoming cracked and George increasingly confused. He beckoned to locals passing by on donkeys or in minibuses, who confirmed that we were on track.

Then, in all modesty, Nebi Uri appeared. Almost lost in its meadow, it is home to the shrine of Uriah the Hittite. Uriah was a brilliant general of the Hittite empire who, around 1000 BCE, went to work for the Israelite King David. It was not a good move. The Old Testament monarch had the commander killed so that he could marry his beautiful wife, Bathsheba. Quite why the wronged Uriah became a figure of religious devotion is lost in the mists of time but stepping into the Roman tower that today stands over his shrine is like stepping back into religious pre-history. Even on a mid-week afternoon, the place was full of Christians, Muslims, Kurds, Armenians and Arabs, praying as they placed pebbles in walls and tied ribbons to trees. Alongside was a mosque, the walls of which were occasionally stained with the blood of slaughtered animals: it was presumably erected to stamp some authority on the heterodox feelings these sacrifices represent.

I had wanted to see Nebi Uri for its mix of visitors and their spiritual connectedness. It embodies a thriving, grassroots syncretism that, in the contemporary Middle East, is almost unique to Syria. It did not disappoint. And it comes to mind, like a counterfactual hope and possibility, whenever I hear of the deadly divisions in the countries that are its neighbours.

11

'Grub first, then ethics.'

Bertolt Brecht

Abraham Maslow is a psychologist, famous for his 'Hierarchy of Human Needs', in which he articulated an idea that, like Freud's notion of the ego or Marx's alienation, has become part of the furniture of modern thought. After Maslow, to say that 'I have needs' is tantamount to a claim of human rights. The expression now carries the meaning that whatever these needs are, they are non-negotiable.

According to Maslow's theory, some human needs are innate, though they may be felt more or less powerfully. These needs are therefore arranged in a hierarchy, usually presented as a horizontally-sliced equilateral triangle, with the needs in the lower segments being more basic and powerful. Those in higher slices might be less potent but they are more distinctive of what it means to be human.

The bottom layer represents physiological needs, such as food, without which we die. The second layer carries the need to be safe and secure, qualities that also indicate the human desire for order and social structure. Third comes the need to belong, manifest in the need for family, friends, lovers and a social group. Fourth are needs to do with esteem, both in the sense of acceptance and status. Without such esteem, people rapidly become despondent; a chronic lack can lead to death almost as surely as being starved of air. At the apex of the pyramid, on the fifth level, is self-actualisation. This differs from the other needs, in that it can never be completely fulfilled, for it is always possible for human beings to imagine more that they might create or achieve. Viktor Frankl, in *Man's Search for Meaning*, added that self-actualisation is also not the same as the call to express oneself; he argues that an individual's greatest potential is achieved by transcending their own narrow existence altogether:

> The true meaning of life is to be found in the world rather than within people or their psyche, as though it were a closed system ... Human experience is, essentially, self-transcendence rather than self-actualisation. Self-actualisation is not really a possible aim, for the simple reason that the more a person strives for it, the more they miss it ... In other words, self-actualisation cannot be attained if it is made an end in itself but only as a side effect of self-transcendence.

This is an important qualifier to a second idea derived from Maslow's hierarchy, which has also gained wide currency. It is often assumed that self-actualisation is a 'peak experience' – an experience that lifts us out of the usual sense of ourselves to provide a universal feeling of meaning. So-called religious peak experiences, like transcendental meditation or charismatic ecstasy, apparently provide obvious examples but Frankl's qualifier calls them into question. He points out that when these states are pursued for their own sake, they do not bring the satisfaction that is sought. The mystics of the great religions say the same: union with the divine is desirable not for the feeling it brings but for the union's spiritual worth.

What has this to do with food? My gripe is with the industrial production of food, typified by mega-supermarkets. In the sense that humanity needs a lot of it, food clearly needs to be produced on an industrial scale but it seems that whether it be eggs from battery hens or unripe (and unripenable) tomatoes, quantity has become the enemy of quality. Tastiness being costly, market forces are usually blamed for this state of affairs. However, people have to be persuaded that food should be cheap to start with. We are prepared to spend a fortune on gizmos and houses. Why not a bit more on food?

I blame Abraham Maslow, for putting food on the lowest rung of the ladder. His move makes us think of food as one of those needs that should cost us almost nothing it is so basic; and since the move from basic to base is a small one, it is easy to think of food as mostly merely a question of sustenance.

There is a deep need to feed the one-third of the human race that lives on or below the breadline and there is also plenty of evidence, from the celebrity chefs to farmers' markets, that people are prepared to pay for food that does more than just fill them up. However, this is surely compensatory behaviour, exceptional and is hardly surprising when so much food, in particular the so-called staples, is so bland. To misquote the sage of the free market, Adam Smith, man is the only animal who is possessed of such niceties that the very taste of what is eaten can hurt him.

I am not seeking endless quantities of the finest fare morning, noon and night. Socrates commented that those who bought food out of season, at an extravagant price, revealed a fear that they would not live until the proper season came round again: 'Eat drink and be merry, for tomorrow we die', is a barely concealed death wish.

Instead, here is a parable. A friend of mine is a bachelor boy, the sort who never cooks and rarely eats at home. His kitchen is empty, save for a few plates and a microwave oven. Having plenty of money, he doesn't just grab a sandwich on the way to work or fish'n'chips on the way home. He eats very well; in fancy coffee bars in the morning, pleasant diners at lunchtime and smart restaurants by night. One day, as a result of an unusual away-day, concocted by his senior manager to nurture thinking 'out of the box', he found himself in a monastery. The morning and afternoon were filled with seminars and sessions, of which my friend remembers little. But what he does recall was the food: not because it was fancy nor because it was foul but because he paid attention to it. At lunchtime, they were served soup. For the first time in many years, he said, he truly ate – in the sense of savouring his food in all its simplicity.

This is what Brecht was talking about. 'Grub first, then ethics' is not meant to be derogatory of ethics, as if there is no time for such niceties when sustenance is the matter in hand. The German word he uses in *The Threepenny Opera* is grub in the sense of 'animal feed', not 'good pub grub'. In other words, we put food below ethics – low down in our life – at the cost of our humanity.

12

'We do not look in great cities for our best morality.'

Jane Austen

Two tales of one city.

The city is London, the place in which Samuel Johnson famously said there is 'all that life can afford'. The first tale is of my move there. I had been working in the north-east of England, in an industrial conurbation chiefly known for its massive chemical works, where I had lived in an old stone cottage, with charm in its undulating walls and sloping floors. Nonetheless, I found the place depressing. It seemed to me that there were no corners to turn and be surprised, no people to meet and be taken out of yourself. To say this is, of course, to comment on myself. It was my imagination or lack of it which necessitated my move south.

London did not disappoint. I think it was the writer Will Self who commented that the definition of a great city is a place that is impossible to grasp in a single thought. Like the event horizons that cosmologists tell us separate our universe from the multi-verse, a city is full of boundaries to step over and places where the laws of possibility have shifted. There is a liberating anonymity, which has always drawn diverse groups; immigrants, gays, malcontents. The ties of obligation that dominate in a parochial setting are replaced by ties of choice: among new friends individuals can reinvent themselves, free of the families and neighbours for whom things will always be the same. To come to London was alchemy.

The second tale is set ten years later. I am sitting upstairs on the bus: it is mid-week and mid-morning, the best time to move through the city; the rush-hour has passed and those who travel now have the time to do it. But this week is the school half-term holiday; the seats at the back of the bus are filled by a bunch of teenage girls, who are rapidly becoming louder and rowdier. I only half-notice them, until I see one of them lift her shirt and press her breasts to the window by her seat.

After a couple of seconds, *en masse* the group moves up against the window, spitting and sneering, 'F**king queer!' She does it again and this time they shout, 'F**king paedophile!' I realise what they are up to. The girl is flashing men on the pavement beneath. If they ignore her, the group screams, 'Queer!' If they appreciate the view, the girls yell 'Paedophile!' This might be thought to be just about within the bounds of bawdy behaviour, were it not for the time of day, the youth of the girls and the venom which loaded their shouts. It was unnerving. I pitied their teacher.

The virtue of cities always has the potential to become vile, which Jane Austen had in mind when she made her comment. This ambivalence was written into the philosophy of urban life from the start, when Plato wrote the *Republic*, his study of the ideal city-state, an attempt to describe the social structures that would make for a happy city life. Plato takes it for granted that such an existence must be found in a city, since all life is there. But he also knows that cities are constantly threatened by division, because the hopes they inspire can easily fail. With that breakdown comes first individual alienation and then warring factions.

Plato's solution is radical: the city is divided into two groups; those who rule, called the guardians and those who work, the holders of wealth. Guardians devote their life to the common good – which might seem laudable and in Plato's scheme they spend much of their time struggling to understand what is good, not least in the pursuit of his metaphysical theory of Forms. However their devotion to the common good necessitates Draconian sanctions on their way of life. The most striking is that they must hold all things in common, from possessions to children. Also, guardians may not have particular friends because that might lead to particular enmities: they must quench their desire for special intimacies as well as their fear of strangers.

The strictures of living in Plato's city are compounded when considering the role of the workers. They cannot play any part in ruling the city because, Plato presumes, their economic interests would inevitably lead them to be swayed by self-interest. This would then undermine the efforts to forge peace and unity in the city. In short, democracy is forbidden as mob rule by another name; oligarchy is endorsed and stands or falls on the abilities of the ruling few.

All in all, the *Republic* would be a hideous place in which to live. Perhaps that is Plato's point. It suggests something that has to be accepted about life in any real city: it trades individual liberty for social civility. Too many laws and all of life would not be there; too few and it becomes uncivil. The question is where the balance lies.

It is probably never possible to strike the balance right though perhaps today things are seriously off-kilter. Road-rage is a key indicator, because the car can be thought of as a place in which liberty and civility collide. I have lived in two parts of London, one relatively poor and the other relatively posh; in both, it is rare to travel anywhere without witnessing or being part of a road-rage incident. Often these incidents are trivial, leading only to the impatient tooting of horns; sometimes they are more serious, with words or blows exchanged. A diffuse aggression seems to be the price we pay for driving in the city and similarly perhaps, also for living there.

Maybe living in a city is like taking a drug. Very often the drug has the effect of the caffeine contained in coffee; it is complex on the tongue and energising to the mind. But on occasion it is like crack, tense with an effect that smacks you between the eyes. Sometimes, everyone should come off cities: if they can.

13

'One cat always leads to another.'

Ernest Hemingway

The great essayist, Michel de Montaigne, asked many questions of life but he asked one that I used to think discredited him. 'When I play with my cat, who knows whether she isn't amusing herself with me more than I am with her?' I thought that the sentimental undercurrent of Montaigne's musing belonged to pet magazines, not philosophy. Until I started sharing my flat with a cat.

Mandalay came into my life via a friend. She had a Burmese cat, Mimbu, which in terms of its behaviour seemed to be a perfect combination of canine friendliness and feline independence. Mimbu would gratifyingly greet my friend at the front door when she came home but was conveniently happy to be left for a night, even two, should she need to be away. Mimbu had kittens. The tumbling bronze ball of wool that was the young Mandalay seemed an ideal addition to the life of a single – as I then was – metrosexual. Affection without overbearing commitment. They even use the litter tray from birth.

'A dog is for life, not just for Christmas', as the advert says: a statement also true of cats. The intimation that there was going to be more to this relationship than I anticipated came as I put Mandalay into her shiny new cat box to take her to her new home. I told my friend that I felt a little cruel taking the kitten away from her brothers and sisters, ending the fun-filled bliss of her first twelve weeks, solely that she might amuse me. My friend replied with a knowing smile: 'You're going to become her significant other now.' Could a cat make such demands? Might she change me?

She did. I noticed immediately how she enlivened my bachelor pad. It was not just that she came to the front door when I returned but during the day, as I worked and she slept, her presence expanded my perception of home. A new kitchen appliance is just another smart accoutrement; a Kelim rug an additional, if beautiful, *objet*. Mandalay, however, was a living creature. There was another spirit about the place. She brought pleasure and concerns. She warmed my heart.

Now for the really sentimental part: within six months of having Mandalay, I met the person with whom I now live. Something that had eluded me for thirty-five years – a committed relationship – materialised, relatively speaking, almost overnight. My response? Ostensibly as a playmate for Mandalay, I bought a second cat. One cat always leads to another.

I now see that Montaigne's question is perfectly valid: what is the nature of the relationship between us and our pets? It is far more than functional: there were no mice to catch in my flat and though a dog may encourage its owner to take more exercise, it brings far more than a healthier way of life. But is it right to call the relationship friendship?

Thorstein Veblen, who wryly put his finger on the materialism of the modern leisured classes by inventing the expression 'conspicuous consumption', thought that keeping domestic animals, which served little functional purpose, was to do with wealth and display. For him, having a cat is essentially the same as owning an expensive racehorse. The purpose of having beautiful creatures in one's possession is to create resentment in one's neighbours; an elegant feline posing on the *chaise longue* is a representation of one's own enviable elegance.

For the owner of Burmese cats – 'posh pussies', as they have been called – there is something in this. However, Veblen notes that cats do not generate as deep an envious response as do the other animals people can have, such as dogs, parrots or horses. He puts this down to the feline temperament. The cat 'lives with man on terms of equality,' he says – hence the superior attitude that many attribute to cats: they do not simply adorn the *chaise longue* but apparently own it, which detracts from, not enhances, the real owner's status. All cat owners have the sense, from time to time, that they are not the master of their own house.

Ambivalence about felines extends to their nature, as well as to the nature of our relationships with them. Cats can exhibit a shocking juxtaposition of great affection and horrid cruelty. Mandalay, for example, will come when you call. She talks to you. She will fetch sticks. She will nuzzle with her head, curl up on your lap and insist on attention. Once, I was standing reading a book and hadn't noticed her rubbing against my legs: to be close to me, she leapt clean through the gap between my body, arms and book to land on my shoulder. She will even indulge me when I want to play and she, at first, doesn't.

However, I will never forget the first time she brought a fledgling blackbird into the house. Like a scene of routine violence from a gangland thriller, it flapped across the floor, trailing a smear of blood; one wing sticking out like a set-square, panting in between its screams. To end its misery, I shovelled it into a carrier bag as Mandalay looked on impassively. My cat was a killer. Worse, a torturing killer. I put it down to instinct but have never worked out what to make of it.

Cats play with us on many levels – literally, emotionally, materially, psychologically. Little wonder the ancient Egyptians worshipped them and embodied the riddles of existence in a creature that was half-feline: the sphinx.

14

'Haste is universal because everyone is in flight from themselves.'

Nietzsche

Newton was right. Everything continues in a state of steady motion unless acted upon by some external force, when they continue to move, only differently. I have just walked to the newspaper shop and back. I passed a young mum pushing a buggy: her child was in agitated motion, a force causing her to accelerate in the rush to reach home before his cries got out of control. Two men in suits were waiting at the bus stop. They were motionless, in that they were not drawing any nearer to their destination and yet still they moved, rocking from foot to foot to quell their impatience at the delay. Someone else, in baggy, carefree clothes, looked in less of a hurry but he too moved, to the sound of music in his ears. Only one man, seated on the wall by the church, with a brown face like a pickled walnut, appeared not to move. Then I saw him reach behind a brick and retrieve a can of beer. He too was on the move, to oblivion.

Like sharks that must swim or drown, stillness seems unnatural. Newton drew on Descartes, who thought movement was divine: 'In the beginning God created matter, along with its motion and rest and now ... he conserves the same quantity of motion in the universe as he put there in the beginning.' This law of the conservation of motion was deduced from Descartes' meditation on heaven: like the celestial spheres, the Earth also will ceaselessly turn. (Though there is a hint of our fallen state in this too; Adam's punishment was ceaseless toil.) This makes one think of Freud, who identified another source of perpetual kinetics, the unconscious. The unconscious is like the swirling of the magma beneath the Earth's crust; there is heat in there and it wants to get out. It is the reason for the slipping and sliding of our emotional lives and is often revealed in unconscious movements. Freud described what happened to one of his patients, Mr R:

> While he talked like this, he would get up from the sofa and roam about the room, a habit which he explained at first as being due to delicacy of feeling: he could not bring himself, he said, to utter such horrible things while he was lying there so comfortably. But soon he himself found a more cogent explanation, namely, that he was avoiding my proximity for fear of my giving him a beating. If he stayed on the sofa he behaved like someone in desperate terror trying to save himself from castigation of terrific violence; he would bury his head in his hands, cover his face with his arm, jump up and suddenly rush away, his features distorted with pain.

All that motion, yet beyond a vague sense of horror and fear, Mr R did not know why he did it, although later in his analysis he remembered that his father used to lose his temper and not know when to stop.

Modern cosmology tells us that it is only as the universe dies that it will approach rest, asymptotically. Like the chill of a cold room that seeps into your bones no matter how much you wrap up, the zillion atoms of the universe will tend towards equilibrium, continually cooling in tandem with the ever-expanding cosmic horizon. But even at infinity, residual oscillations will remain, like an echo of the activity that once powered stars – and intelligence.

Often, motion is a blessing. Some have argued that a human being's rational nature can be thought of as in motion, progressing irresistibly forward, if sometimes rather erratically. If that positive spin seems less plausible today, the indisputable case of motion as a great good must be music, an impossible pleasure unless it proceeds beat by beat, bar by bar. This is why concert-goers and rock fans refuse to let the musicians leave the stage after a brilliant performance: they do not want the moment to pass – though paradoxically, there could be no such moment without the passing.

This is also why portable music, that can be played and repeated, is simultaneously a joy and a threat. If music is listened to continually, it might never be heard, because all that is played is its middle, not its beginning or end. As Daniel Barenboim has pleaded, without the finality of the cadence, without the temporality of the climax, without the silence of the beginning and the end, there is no music. Deny the loss implicit in its movement and you lose the music.

Any meditation on motion must pay its respects to the early thinking of the pre-Socratic philosopher, Heraclitus, for whom flux was the fundamental fact of existence. He compared reality with a river which, because it flows, can never, strictly speaking, be stepped into twice. 'You should quench violence more quickly than a fire,' he said, since the danger of violence is found in its rampant motion. He conceived of the soul as an exhalation: like the body that has two choices, breathe again or expire, the soul is renewed by its rhythm. Even reason cannot get a grip on things unless it has a before and an after to compare and contrast.

The implication is that to be human is to move. Inasmuch as the atoms of your body replace themselves over the weeks and years, this is true. Psychologically it is also true, as anyone who has tried to recall what it was like to be a child will appreciate: you lived a different life then. Philosophers have taken the thought to extremes, wondering whether there can really be such a thing as personal identity, if change is so radical that it disrupts our sense of continuity.

Conversely, motionlessness is taken to be an attribute of divinity. Medieval theologians argued that God cannot change since, if he did, he would have to become either more perfect or less perfect, which as perfection already, he cannot. Similarly, stillness is often taken as a mark of sanctity and wisdom: God is heard in the still, small voice. The mythical Hindi saint, who for days does not move, even to drink, is drawing on the same tradition that tells of the day Socrates stood without moving for so long that by midday a crowd had gathered around him and then more took their beds outside to watch him through the night. They did not suppose he had gone mad, for his stillness, obviously, meant that he was contemplating.

What of Nietzsche's thought? 'Haste is universal, because everyone is in flight from themselves.' He knew his Heraclitus; he believed that nothing stands still. Indeed, he escalated the principle into a doctrine he invented called the eternal recurrence. What his thought suggests is that while it is easier to move faster, become busier or grow more restless because you are on the move already, there is much to be gained from steering away from the strongest currents and finding an eddy that allows you, if not to stop and think, at least to think. If everything is in motion and there is no place of absolute rest, there is the possibility of relative stillness in the chaos. In the words of Saul Bellow, art, like prayer, achieves 'an arrest of attention in the midst of distraction'. More deliberation in your movement, less in flight from yourself.

THE WORKING LIFE

15

'Let's go to work.'

from Quentin Tarantino's Reservoir Dogs

Why do people work? It seems like a question with one clear, quick answer: money. But whilst if few people work for no money – and when they do it is often because they do not much need it – remuneration cannot be the whole story. People spend a great proportion of their lives working. Even if work is a financial necessity, its impact will be felt far more deeply than in the bank. Work accrues meaning to itself. The meaning you derive from work is worth pursuing.

The psychoanalyst, Slavoj Žižek, raises one possibility. It has to do with cleaning – housework, it might be said. He argues that work is surprisingly enjoyable because, perhaps unconsciously, it satisfies the need to keep the ever-encroaching mess of life at bay. Work is the ego bringing superego-like order to libidinal chaos, as the straight furrows of the ploughed field bring symmetry to a wild stretch of land. The tidy folders in the filing cabinet make sense of otherwise disorientating information. Most of life is not amenable to this tidying. So where it is, in the limited tasks we are asked to do for a living, it brings a profound sense of contentment.

A second option for the meaning of work was advocated by the Victorian essayist, Thomas Carlyle. He said that work should not be merely a matter of earning a living; the 'cash nexus', as he called it. As Karl Marx was to show more thoroughly in his theory of alienation, Carlyle thought work should not be so humiliating but should provide individuals with a sense of identity and purpose, offering them a social and moral framework. To work is to find purpose:

> Blessed is he who has found his work; let him ask no other blessedness. He has a work, a life-purpose; he has found it and will follow it! ... Labour is Life: from the inmost heart of the Worker rises his God-given Force, the sacred celestial Life-essence breathed into him by Almighty God; from his inmost heart awakens him to all nobleness, to all knowledge, 'self-knowledge' and much else, so soon as Work fitly begins.

Others have said that work justifies what you have in life. For the Ancient Greeks, work that produced things – food, buildings, shoes, clothes or medical care – was menial. 'Citizens must not lead the life of artisans or tradesmen, for such a life is ignoble and inimical to excellence,' wrote Aristotle in his *Politics*; 'Neither must they be farmers, since leisure is necessary both for the development of excellence and the performance of political duties.' He had a point. How many people routinely collapse from office exhaustion at the end of every day? How many drink away their wages on a Friday night, because their work is drudgery? Their work may well have no meaning; rather, it has become a palliative to unhappiness or boredom.

The ancient ideals of the aristocratic life of cultivated leisure faded in the sixteenth century. Reformers, such as Luther, thought the inactive body was too open to vice. Morrisey's lyric – 'the devil will find work for idle hands to do', which led him to steal and lie – is an almost direct repeat of a proverb from this period. The Protestant Work Ethic completed the transformation, turning work into a public virtue, because it improves the individual and contributes to society. The economic significance of that was formalised by John Locke. As labour transforms the earth into something usable, so labour transforms what is worthless into something valuable. That value is then the property of the labourer: 'The Labour of his Body and the Work of his Hands, we may say, are properly his.' To work is to have status; hence the social stigma attached to unemployment and the prestige attached to highly paid work.

Whatever meaning is attributed to work, at a personal level the problem is that it demands so much of a person's time. People are, inevitably, not just preoccupied with it but shaped by it, down to the level of their character. 'Man is a creature who makes pictures of himself and then comes to resemble those pictures,' wrote Iris Murdoch. The Cockney slang for a 'merchant banker' is not just an accidental rhyme. Saint Benedict, the writer of the famous monastic rule, realised this. The labour his monks engaged in, day by day, contributed as much to their spiritual formation as did the explicitly religious aspects of monastic life such as reading the Bible or saying the Office. Work was not just a question of getting things done. It determined the kind of people they were becoming, be that holy or grumpy (a trait with which Benedict seems to have been particularly concerned). He identified what might be called good work; work which builds the individual up, body and soul. Interestingly, he particularly addresses the matter in the vow of obedience. His point is that everyone obeys something or someone, never more so than when at work. The question is whether that obedience is liberating. Bad work, like the sweat shop, is dehumanising and enslaving; good work nurtures the individual positively.

'We know that it is by this way of obedience that we go to God,' wrote Benedict. Transcribed into a secular idiom, this means you make the most of the limited freedom you have in work. Within the constraints you face, choose your job – choose who you are obeying – well. It is a choice that not only revolves around the pay packet but also to the extent to which it cultivates your character and inculcates a sense of meaning. To recall another line from a song: it's not just nice work, if you can get it, but good work that counts.

16

'Freedom and slavery are mental states.'

Gandhi

Freedom is a refrain constantly in the air. Politicians declaim it. Pop stars sing about it. Philosophers discuss it. So what, exactly, is it? Three definitions that I have recently come across:

First, the current political orthodoxy that freedom is choice: the more choices you have, the more freedom you enjoy. The advantage of this definition is that it aspires to leave the pursuit of freedom up to individuals. The disadvantage is that it tends to make choice an end in itself.

Second, freedom is equality: the more equality of opportunity there is in the world, the more freedom is enjoyed by all. The advantage of this definition is that it addresses the inequalities that remove freedoms from the poor and minorities. The disadvantage is that it tends to see freedom in material terms, whereas freedom is far more than that, as Gandhi pointed out.

Third, a suggestion that at first, seems bizarre: freedom is obedience. The advantage of this definition is that it is not fooled by the marketplace that dresses up the consumer's choice to buy this or that as freedom: it understands the world as a place in which everyone obeys rules, whether they like it or not, so they might as well choose the best rules there are – the ones that aim for the good life – and follow them. The disadvantage of this suggestion is that it is not at all clear where the rules that are good to obey are to be found.

To these three, I will add one more – not a full-blooded theory of freedom so much as a test as to whether you are walking in the direction of more or less freedom. The test is friendship. For it seems to me that the better the quality of your friendships – in terms of honesty, shared life, compassion and love of life – the more your life is likely to be genuinely free.

17

'Money can't buy you happiness but it does buy a more pleasant form of misery.'

Spike Milligan

The dangers of money are well rehearsed in philosophy:

'You cannot serve God and Mammon,' said Jesus, knowing that people often end up working for money in more senses than one.

'Money is like muck, not good except it be spread,' warned Francis Bacon, in a phrase that explains everything from the showy ostentation of the *nouveau riche*, to the social unrest that stems from the divide between rich and poor.

'Money is indeed the most important thing in the world; and all sound and successful personal and national morality should have this fact for its basis,' wrote George Bernard Shaw ominously.

Let us narrow our horizons. 'Money couldn't buy friends but you got a better class of enemy,' Spike Milligan said, in another place. What is it with friendship and money?

Aristotle told a story about a guitarist who played at a rich man's party. He was contracted to play for so many hours for so much money. However, his playing was so beautiful that the party-giver asked him to play some more, which the guitarist did, from goodwill. That night, with the music lifting everyone out of themselves and uniting them in its magic, it was as if the musician and the host had become friends.

The next morning the guitarist asked for his money, thinking he deserved more for playing more. He was primarily there to earn a living. The party-giver, however, did not see it that way. He thought the guitarist had played more for friendship's sake. Moreover, he could not understand why playing so wonderfully was not reward enough.

The guitarist wanted cash; the party-giver a fine pleasure. The nascent friendship crashed. Money failed to bridge the gap, indeed left it gaping wider.

Friendliness as an accompaniment to everyday commercial transactions should be unproblematic. When I pay so much for a pair of shoes, continued Aristotle, I know what the price is and I just pay up; not jeopardising the friendliness I can offer the shoemaker. The amount of friendliness between strangers on the high street is indeed quite remarkable. Currency is a measure, a means to an end, Aristotle explained. When it accurately reflects the cost of what is exchanged, people are free to be friendly in addition to the commerce.

The problem comes when money is an inadequate expression of what someone gives and another receives or think they have given or received. Protagoras, the sophist, used to ask for money for his teaching. He asked to be paid according to the worth his students felt his teaching had. Socrates thought this was a category error: how can wisdom be allotted a financial value? So, he did not charge.

This is why money is so dangerous to friendship. Friendship deals in a currency that money does not understand. The risk, for friends, is that an exchange of money for a service rendered might call into question other values in the relationship. It is as if an accountant has become involved: no longer can you give and not count the cost. When generosity is priced up, it is as if the cash claws all value – not just financial – to itself.

The solution is to undermine money with generosity, to combat accounting with giving. This is what Aristotle's party-giver failed to do the morning after the night before. He should have paid the guitarist double the money and more; he could afford it. The guitarist would then have been in a position to be generous in return. With their debts more than discharged, a new friendship could have taken their relationship forward. 'Friends do not put the scales centre stage,' Aristotle concluded.

18

'You must want nothing if you wish to challenge Jupiter, who himself wants nothing.'

Seneca

Socrates was famous for his austerity. For much of his life he was better known for not wearing shoes than for the thoughts he uttered. There is a story that one day he went to the marketplace. Crowds jostled and trestles bowed with goods from across the Mediterranean. A trader spotted Socrates and, amused by the thought of selling something to the man who sported nothing, yelled: 'What will you buy? What do you lack?'

Socrates turned to look. He longed, with passion, for something he lacked. His desire for it haunted him; it drove his way of life. The question was arresting but what did he seek? Only wisdom – worth more than all the gold of Darius.

There is not a single character of any substance in Plato's dialogues who did not sometimes find Socrates difficult. Some of his fellow citizens occasionally slapped him about the face – literally – in their rage against his high-mindedness. His desire for wisdom made them feel uncomfortable; it exposed the paucity of their own pursuits. They added a kick to their slaps, for good measure. He apparently forgave them, albeit with a quip – 'Kicking is what asses do.' He understood that his own discontent awakened theirs. All mortals are in the same boat, he realised; neither he nor they could live like the gods, wanting nothing.

Socrates was no puritan: he loved feasts and drinking. Another story that did the rounds was that he could drink all night and yet stay sober, a trick that seemed like sorcery to his companions. Perhaps his imperviousness to the effects of alcohol was a metaphor: the man who seeks to escape life drinks to get drunk, unlike the man who drinks in all that life offers in his search for wisdom.

So, the stallholder called out. Possibly some of the shoppers nearby turned to hear how Socrates would respond. Would he be sympathetic or would he cut the trader down to size?

Socrates went up to the stall, took in all the goods before him and spread his hands before its plenty. 'Good gods!' he cried. 'Who would have thought there were so many things in the world that I did not want!'

19

'The soul is the prison of the body.'

Michel Foucault

Glass waves, glass shards, glass curves. Glass has replaced concrete as the material that signifies a building is modern. But glass also resonates with our times for more opaque reasons.

There is a block of flats in London, on the southern end of Lambeth Bridge. Known as Parliament View, it features in Woody Allen's film *Match Point* as the first home of two newly-weds. It is made of glass. This is not particularly striking; nearly all the bridges of central London have gathered clusters of glass buildings around them. The walls of these buildings are transparent. You can see into each room and look directly at what people are doing. It is as if the flats were theatre sets or stacks of cardboard boxes with the open ends exposed to the world. As you cross Lambeth and the other bridges, you see televisions being watched, beds being made, suppers being eaten.

The first time I noticed these lives being lived so visibly I was astonished. Glass may be appealing for the light it allows in and the views it yields but surely buyers would draw a line at being so exposed. To live there would be like living in a goldfish bowl or under twenty-four hour surveillance. Then I thought again. Perhaps this is precisely the life the residents seek. Like a model on a catwalk, they want their model urban lives to draw the eye and be watched. And then I thought one more time. Perhaps, in a peculiar way, being watched not only makes them feel glamorous but also as if their lives have meaning.

In the eighteenth century, Jeremy Bentham, the great utilitarian philosopher, devised a new plan for prisons. These prisons were to be circular, with the cells built around the circumference. Each cell extended the full depth of the building and was lit by an inner and an outer window. The space the cells enclosed was empty, save for a tower at its centre. In the tower sat an observer, who monitored the behaviour of the 'backlit' prisoners. Bentham called the building the Panopticon.

It was crucial to Bentham's design that the observer could not be seen: the tower had Venetian blinds and its staircases and corridors were maze-like, to prevent the noise of the guards moving about inside reaching the prisoners. The theory was that the prisoners could be continually observed but that they could not tell if they were or were not. The goal was that, over the period of their sentence, they would internalise this invisible observation, leading them to develop fixed habits of monitoring themselves. This self-disciplining and self-monitoring would achieve each prisoner's reform and renew their sense of purpose.

A handful of such prisons were built, though the struggle to get the design accepted almost bankrupted Bentham. And it was not until the twentieth century that Michel Foucault spotted how the Panopticon had succeeded in a way that Bentham could never have envisaged.

Its first indirect success was the development of the modern penal system. One of the characteristics of the early reforms was that corporal punishment, the punishment of the body, was replaced by incarceration, the punishment of the whole person. In Jake Arnott's novel *The Long Firm*, Harry, a brutal, imprisoned gang leader, reads Foucault while serving his sentence. It captures this change and what it is like to experience it exactly. Harry explains to a friend:

> When you're banged up you're allowed to exercise, you can study and pretend you're not turning into a zombie. But all along your personality, that delicate sense of freedom and integrity, is constantly being exercised and disciplined in time and space. That's the soul. The effect and instrument of a political anatomy. They imprison it, it imprisons you. The soul is the prison of the body.

Harry is complaining about how invasive the modern penal system is, more invasive than even convicted criminals deserve. Whatever the truth of that, Foucault thought that the panoptic principle did not stop at the prison gates. He thought that what had been a design for a building had become an idea around which to build a society. A system of rules and laws had been constructed, which leads not just prisoners but also citizens, to think they are being observed.

Scientific advances played a key part. During the nineteenth century, theories of deviancy – what was normal and abnormal – that had never existed before, became commonplace. Once introduced, people came to judge themselves according to those theories. They read about insanity and asked themselves whether they were sane; they read about homosexuality and asked whether they were gay or straight. The self-critique extended to all parts of life, to clothes, to manners, to eating habits – the stuff of everyday existence: these were the things that signified whether you were crossing the lines of acceptability. There were no police to enforce the right behaviour: scientific experts, political correctness, public opinion and above all the person themself took the role of the hidden, panoptic observer. Foucault put it this way:

> No need for arms, physical violence or material restraints. Just an observing gaze that each individual feels weighing on him and ends up internalising to the point that he is his own overseer: everyone in this way exercises surveillance over and against himself.

What has this to do with the glass apartment blocks on London's bridges? Foucault argued that the reason people are not only prepared to put up with this surveillance but also to welcome it is fear – a fear that emerged with the Enlightenment, the intellectual movement that vowed no corner of human experience would escape the light of reason, implying that which is thereby illuminated is meaningful, because it is understood. Conversely, that which remains obscure and dark, because it is not amenable to rational analysis, seems meaningless, even dangerous.

Couple this bipolar thinking to the panoptic mentality and, in the name of security, the duty of every human being becomes the duty of surveillance, to light themselves and the world around them. This is why most are happy to live in a surveyed society: CCTV cameras are a reasonable step. They make people feel safe.

Better still to live in the light, in a glass-sided building. It is modern, it is illuminated, it is observed, it is meaningful. Thus, presumably, the inhabitants of Parliament View do not think they live in a goldfish bowl. They think they live in a highly desirable residence.

THE SOCIAL LIFE

20

'The desire for friendship comes quickly.
Friendship does not.'

Aristotle

Can friendship be taught? More strongly, should it be? There are good reasons to think it should.

First, friendship matters to people more than most things in life. They agree with Aristotle that a life without friendship is no life. Think of the training people receive in the pursuit of money: would it not make sense to put some time into developing the capacity for friendship?

Second, there is the intimate connection between friendship and a healthy society. Plato noted that nothing is more fundamental to the well-being of society than the absence of enmity, because nothing is more fearsome to society than civil strife. He argued that friendship should be a required virtue of those who govern. This suggestion should not be dismissed idly; civil war and international strife are terrible things. Moreover, so-called political friendships are routinely betrayed, with disastrous consequences. Those who are not with us are against us, say the leaders of the free world, a doctrine that makes friendship a matter of expedience. It is based not on the optimism of shared aspirations but on the cynicism of shared enemies.

Third, look at the greatest sources of wisdom on friendship; the writings of the ancient Greeks and Romans. They were written with didactic aims. Plato's dialogue on friendship, the *Lysis*, is a model conversation on amity that served as a launch pad for debate among the students of his Academy; Aristotle's books on friendship, found in the *Nicomachean Ethics*, are a collection of lecture notes; Cicero's piece, the *Laelius*, was written in a vain attempt to educate the elite of the late Roman republic; and Seneca's letters on friendship were sent to instruct a friend. Today, there is plenty written about friendship but it is presented as explorations or portrayals in novels or films. Perhaps we should take a leaf out of the works of the ancients and be unashamedly programmatic?

What would they teach us? Aristotle thought there were three types of friendship. First, there are friendships of utility, friendships which form because of something that is done together. Work friends are an obvious example. Such comradeship, be it during the lunch break or in the meeting room, undoubtedly contributes to the greater happiness of millions but it is flawed. It tends to last only so long as the thing done together lasts and the amity it nurtures tends to be ephemeral. That is why even a work friendship of many years' standing will fizzle out when one of the friends moves office or changes job.

Aristotle's second type of friendships is those of pleasure, formed because of something that is enjoyed together. These friendships mirror those based on something that is done together and they share the same flaw. Consider sexual relationships: though they may come to find wellsprings in the meeting of souls as well as of bodies, the friendship that lovers share is challenged when the sex subsides and no other source of love is found. With a nod to teenage psychology, Aristotle notes that such pleasure-friendship is particularly common among young people. As their pleasures can change many times, even within one day, he writes, so may not their friends? From sex – or pleasures from football to fashion – these friendships carry the same risk: without the pleasure, the friendship flounders. Lord Byron, the Romantic's Don Juan, by his own confession wandered in 'lonely woods'.

The third kind of friendship is different and is the best. Aristotle variously calls it friendship of character, virtue or excellence. In a more modern idiom, such lucky individuals might be called soulmates or best friends. Friends of this sort love each other because of who they are in themselves: their friendship does not depend upon an external thing like work or pleasure. Because their quality is their good character, virtue or excellence (and because these good things last), this kind of friendship is not only the best but the most longlasting.

With his schema explained, Aristotle proceeded to instruct his students in the ups and downs of real friendships. Friends need to be equals, he said. Should one friend become far richer than another, this will threaten the friendship, because the rich friend will feel the need to offer largesse and the poorer may be tempted to make requests. Aristotle also highlighted the centrality of meaningful communication: 'Cut off the talk and many times you cut off the friendship.' He advocated friends living together – not necessarily living under one roof but sharing many of life's activities (his list includes drinking, playing dice, hunting and philosophising). Friends who only speak once in a while, perhaps by email or phone, risk finding that they have become strangers to one another and friends who only meet at reunions are probably on a nostalgia trip – another form of pleasure.

One of the most profound moments in Aristotle's friendship lecture comes a little over halfway through. 'A friend is another self,' he said. He meant this in two ways: first, friends are another self to each another, since they see themselves in each other. They know each other. A shorthand for the love called friendship can be derived from this insight: if the love of families is characterised by the desire to care and be cared for and the love between lovers is characterised by the desire to have and be had, the love shared by friends is characterised by the desire to know the other and be known by them.

Second, in saying that a friend is another self Aristotle is suggesting something deeper. He is pondering the idea that an individual's sense of who they are is caught up in friendship. Perhaps he had in mind a comment of Philoctetes, in Sophocles' play. This unfortunate Greek prince, famous for a foul-smelling wound in his foot, was left on a desert island for ten years. During that time he described himself as 'a corpse among the living' and he did not mean it metaphorically. To the modern mind, to be friendless is to be sad, lonely or vulnerable but not dead. This is because autonomy – that great but isolating virtue – is what we would say is essential to being human. Aristotle, however, would have taught something that profoundly challenges that notion. You cannot find yourself without friendship. Perhaps there is an echo of that when someone says they basked in the reflected glory of their friend. Not only are they glad for their friend but also they received a boost to their own sense of self.

Aristotle also taught about the ending of friendships. This can happen because people change, do bad things or move on. His advice is always to sever the friendship only after due time and thought. This is partly because worst enemies were often once best friends. More positively, he thinks that a good friend is one of life's great blessings and so the friendship deserves reverence even when spoiled. Nietzsche took this point very seriously. He called broken friendships 'star friendships': like a star, you should enjoy the light of past friendships without them casting a continuing shadow over you.

Can friendship be taught? Should it be? In one sense yes, because there is much advice to impart. Arguably, any friendship might be improved by that and the best kinds of friendship will be both better recognised and better valued. However, the teaching of friendship has its limits: like a self-help book cannot guarantee happiness, no one can be instructed into friendship.

Plato should have the last word on this. He did not give lectures on friendship, as far as we know, but constructed a dialogue using the clever device of friends talking about friendship. The brilliance of this approach is that the friends can be observed being challenged and their friendship being deepened as their conversation progresses. They don't just talk friendship, they make friends. The exchange ends inconclusively: the friends cannot say what friendship is and the conversation is passed over to the dialogue's readers. The message is clear. Teaching can identify conditions and complexities. But ultimately, friendship is discovered and understood only with friends.

21

'Never do to others what you would not like them to do to you.'

Confucius

It was well into the evening, fine wine was flowing and we had before us one of those big questions. What is it that the world's religions share in common?

One friend ventured monotheism. She knew, of course, that strictly, only the People of the Book are believers in one God but she argued that there is a unifying divine principle behind all religions. The suggestion lost traction when someone pointed out that some Buddhists do not believe in a God or gods, at all.

A second idea was forgiveness. This person's argument went like this. In paganism, you are tied, by chains of blame, to your past: the Romans dug around in animal entrails to see whether decisions about their future were favourable. But with Christianity, Islam and Judaism the idea came about that you can escape your past – be forgiven – and start life afresh. It was a fascinating idea. Again, unfortunately, it failed because of the concept of karma in Eastern religions. There is no forgiveness there: the past comes back to haunt you.

It was the third idea that held hold: compassion, the golden rule. Confucius, Buddha and the Mahabharata taught it. Allah is merciful. Jesus said to his disciples, 'Love your neighbour as yourself.' Rabbi Hillel summed up the Torah: 'What is hateful to yourself, do not do to your fellow man.'

The principle has found its way to the heart of secular philosophies too. Kant formulated his version in his categorical imperative, the one rule you cannot not disregard: do those things that should be done by all. In a different guise, evolutionary theory has 'reciprocal altruism'; the idea that it is adaptively advantageous to do things for others because they are then more inclined to do things for you.

Having said that, the modern, post-religious versions have changed something in the formula, transforming it from an act of compassion to one of calculation. Evolutionary theorists are the most explicit in this. They consider games, such as the Prisoner's Dilemma, in which one of the most successful strategies for winning is tit-for-tat; whatever you do to me, I do to you. In other words, it is useful to obey the golden rule not because it is good but because it enables you to survive.

Kant's categorical imperative implies a similar moral shift. Take his analysis of friendship: a friend, he says, is someone who you can trust to do what is good for you not because they love you – which they may only do to a degree and not with 100 per cent reliability – but because they, in return, trust you to do what is good for them. According to this understanding, friendship is a pact not that distinct from a mutual scratching of backs. It is not a concern for another. It is actually a concern for yourself. Construed in this way, surely it ceases to be friendship? And the new golden rule seems to be that you should think of others because that turns out to be good for you. 'Tit for tat reprisals make the world go round,' sneered Karl Marx. Or as Oscar Wilde quipped, 'Selfishness is not living as one wishes to live, it is asking others to live as one wishes to live.' Reciprocal altruism's morality is that each person should nurture a secretly selfish selflessness.

It might be thought that this doesn't matter. Friendship is sometimes calculating but as long as we feel useful, not used, we don't mind and are even glad. Only those who engage in logical chicanery or evolutionary casuistry distort compassion irrevocably. Except that the implicit demand – what is in it for me? – seems to resonate with our times.

Let us confront the matter head on. What is in genuine compassion for me? What is lost if it becomes mere calculation? The answer is striking. Not survival or even morality but, in a word, happiness. The Latin root of compassion means to have 'fellow feeling'; it is to put oneself in another person's shoes, to stop asking whether they are friend or foe and to shift perspective and see them as themselves. As Iris Murdoch expressed it, 'Love is the difficult realisation that something other than oneself is real.'

Religious teachers latched on to compassion because they realised that its empathy reaches to another dimension of experience. It steps outside the boundaries of the individual ego to encounter another level of knowing the world. Partly this is sensed in the reward that comes with acts of kindness; it is the reason for the satisfaction of doing something for someone else and partly it is why it is better to give than to receive: a gift celebrates a connection; a gift given liberates the giver from isolation.

So, the quintessence of compassion is not just doing good things for others. It is a state of being – of being and experiencing – from the point of view of others. The self is decentred, expanded, liberated.

At a mundane level, I imagine I sometimes glimpse this when travelling through a suburb on a train. Homes pass by as rapidly as the clickety-clack of the track. Each is a fixed centre of the world for other people, a sun around which everything, for them, revolves. Seeing these hundreds, thousands, of other centres can suddenly dislodge my attention from my own centre, my own view of things. It decentres my sense of self. Conversely, I understand why Buddhism equates egoism with ignorance: self-centredness is a lack of knowledge of other people and things.

At a more exhilarating level, think again of what it means to bask in reflected glory. From your pride at a friend's success to the joy of your side winning, the intensity of the experience increases in direct proportion to the identification with the other person or entity. To bask in reflected glory is, therefore, to practice compassion.

In religious language, the most profound compassion is identifying with the most valuable things that exist, with other human beings and then – if you believe – God. This is also why compassion is presented in the great religions as a source of ultimate value and meaning, because it yields intimations of transcendence.

It is natural to be concerned with survival: tit-for-tat may be good for that. It is human to want to be moral: the categorical imperative is not a bad way of living. But it is divine to be full of compassion.

22

'A gift is something that you cannot be thankful for.'

Jacques Derrida

It is the custom, in the days around the lunar New Year, for the Chinese to give children and single people *lai see* – monetary gifts in bright red packets. Like tinsel at Christmastime, this tawdry stationery can be seen everywhere during January, from outside the temple to inside Starbucks. The invitation is to pop in a few notes and give the envelopes away. What a valuable tradition, one might think, in an otherwise competitive, commercial world.

But the gesture is not wholly generous. For one thing, red packets are to the Chinese what brown envelopes are in the West; they signify a bribe. It's not just the thought that counts: the amount does too. The cash enclosed is in auspicious amounts – often multiples of eight – for this is partly also the meaning of the exchange, namely to impart good luck. The gift is given but it is loaded.

'No surprise in that,' would be the thought of a number of modern philosophers, for the logic of the gift implies nothing else: I give *lai see* to you; you are grateful to me. But therein lies the rub. For you now owe a debt of gratitude to me. In receiving my gift, you have put yourself in debt – my debt. Moreover, I am entitled to feel pleased with myself on account of my generosity. So, in giving, I receive something: self-congratulation. The giver receives; the receiver gives. It is more blessed to give than to receive. As Derrida says, 'A gift is something that you cannot be thankful for.'

This bind might be thought impossible to break. The dinner invitation inevitably leads to an obligation to return the hospitality. The

Christmas card sent one year merely mirrors the greetings in the one received twelve months before. And, no doubt, *lai see* received demands *lai see* to be given.

However, there is one economy that at least loosens the bind of gift-giving: the economy of friendship. I am not talking about the varieties of mere friendliness that ease loneliness and are, thankfully, commonplace (for all that they implicitly demand friendliness in return). Rather, this is friendship as an ideal; being one soul in two bodies, according to Montaigne or exclaiming 'Do you see the same truth?' with Emerson. It is rarely lived, though can be glimpsed: remember Socrates' conclusion in Plato's dialogue on friendship, the *Lysis*: 'We will look foolish, for though we are friends, we have not been able to say what friendship is.'

Aristotle, ever the analytical optimist, had another attempt at defining it. His notion of the friend as 'another self' is particularly rich. The expression is not meant in the trivial sense of friends who enjoy the same pleasures or share the same interests; strangers on the street will do that. Rather, the friend is another self in a dynamic sense. Excellent friends confound the 'I' and 'Thou' that separate the merely friendly and yet preserve them, for they simultaneously remain 'other selves' to each other. The friends exist in a simultaneous state of identification and difference.

From this stems the ethical importance of an ideal of friendship: it is a unique synthesis of self and other love. 'In loving their friend they love what is good for themselves. For the good person, in becoming a friend, becomes a good for the person to whom they become a friend,' Aristotle wrote.

Giorgio Agamben takes it a step further. He argues that Aristotle's concept of the friend as another self is saying more than that friendship is an inter-subjective experience, because that presupposes a prior autonomous subject, alien to Aristotle. Rather, it implies that the very awareness of one's own existence and the awareness of the ideal friend's existence are one and the same thing: 'The friend is not another I but an otherness immanent in self-ness, a becoming other of the self,' he says.

To glimpse the ideal of friendship is therefore also a revelation of the givenness of existence. Its love is created out of nothing. This revelation comes in a distinct guise – the love of another. It is not to experience existence as brute fact but rather to experience existence as gift.

The only response is gratitude.

Here's the final twist: that gratitude is not so much to the friend as with the friend. Friendship perhaps transcends the conundrum of giving and reveals existence as a gift without strings, to boot.

23

'Our friend's electric!'

after the title of a Gary Numan song

The burgeoning world of online relationships has spawned a new verb: 'to friend'. It is what happens when people link up on social websites like MySpace and Facebook. It differs markedly from 'to befriend' which involves getting to know someone. To 'friend' is just to connect. When you friend you do not think of meeting anyone and you can drop a 'friended' friend as quickly as you 'friended' them at the start.

The elimination of the 'be' – friending's ontological deficit – appears to free the individual seeking to friend from all quantitative limitations. There are websites that can friend for you automatically, making your online list of friends look copious – which is vital for friending some more. A worm program provides this multiplication of contacts without any human intervention at all.

It is possible that friending could develop into befriending, although, because it is the quantity of friends that count in the former and the quality of the friendship that counts in the latter, the vast majority of the friended will not become traditional friends. Sheer volume militates against it. To most users of MySpace, a friend list numbered in the thousands seems to be regarded as pretty impressive, in hundreds OK, in tens bad – since it probably means you aren't much capable of friending. Only a few users feel that friend lists of large sizes are spooky.

What is this doing to friendship – to offline, traditional befriending? The sociologist Sherry Turkle has expressed the worry that online living is transforming human psychology, by reducing our ability to be alone and with it the ability to manage and contain our emotions. We are developing new intimacies with machines, which lead to new dependencies – a wired social existence, 'a tethered self'. Conversation becomes a sharing of gossip, photos or profiles, not, on the whole, of the deeper aspects of commitment, community and politics.

Also, although the Internet opens gateways to information, it does not teach much about how to sustain connections or deal with complexity. Even the information can easily be wrong. This distracts from self-reflection and nurtures quick rather than considered responses. This changes one's psychology: do people have their own thoughts? do they have their own autonomy? do they have the skills to find meaning?

The double trouble with the Internet, it seems to me, is that often its freedom is presented precisely as an individual's own thoughts, autonomy and meaning, when actually all these might be merely borrowed – unless you, the individual, take the time offline.

It is hard to resist the analysis of Zygmunt Bauman in his book, *Liquid Fear*. He argues that the collapse of trust has reached such a point that all relationships have become sites of anxiety, not tranquillity. We compensate for a lack of quality in friendship with quantity:

> While unable to put our suspicions to rest and stop sniffing out treachery and fearing frustration, we seek – compulsively and passionately – wider 'networks' of friends and friendship; indeed, as wide a 'network' as we can manage to squeeze into the mobile phone directory that, obligingly, grows more capacious with every new generation of mobiles.

The online age is not the first in which friendship has been made into a commodity but in marginalising the human to such an extent, is it not taking this to a new and frightening level?

24

'Love is blind'.

Anon

Hippothales has a singular distinction. A young Athenian aristocrat, he appears in Plato's dialogue the *Lysis*. And as far as I know, he is the only character in a major philosophical work who features because he has a massive, uncontrollable infatuation.

He is mad about a boy, the statuesque youth, Lysis. His passion is blindingly obvious to everyone around for even the thought of his beloved sparks paroxysms of blushing. 'He's not healthy, he's raving, he's mad,' cries Hippothales' friend, Ctesippus to Socrates, who stops to talk with the two in Plato's story.

Worse, Hippothales looks ridiculous to his friends. Lysis is a model Athenian, shown particularly in his devotion to his family. Wallowing in his obsession, Hippothales resorts to singing songs about the honour and virtue of Lysis' ancestors. If that sounds bizarre, it was annoying to Ctesippus, who begs Hippothales to belt up.

Socrates says this indulgence is ill-judged for a different reason. In singing about Lysis, Hippothales is fooling himself that Lysis is already his. 'You are like a hunter, singing the songs of victory, before you have even started out on the hunt,' says Socrates – adding that if Lysis happened to overhear one of these cringing hymns, then Hippothales would undoubtedly scare him off!

Then, in the dialogue, Lysis himself appears. Like a fainting fan confronted by their pop idol, Hippothales goes to pieces. He hides behind a pillar, begging Socrates not to let on that he is there: the grip that Lysis has on his mind is so potent that to talk to him would be utterly overpowering. This is the thrill of infatuation; it appears to take you out of yourself – it feels like compassion. It is also its psychosis, as Socrates then explains.

In a verbal slap around the face, he tells Hippothales that love – or at least this ridiculous obsession – has made him blind. He does not really know Lysis as an individual. Anyone could tell you he is handsome. Most people know he is devoted to his family. The object of your infatuation, Socrates tells Hippothales, is not the real Lysis but a chimera – an angelic ideal that Hippothales has projected on to the young lad.

Socrates was a generous person. He was frequently infatuated himself (one of his lesser-known distinctions in the history of philosophy is admitting he was once stopped, in full rational flow, by the sight of the gorgeous torso of the hunk Callicles). He offered Hippothales – or any 'infatuand' – three tips, in ascending order of importance:

First, get to know the person concerned. Talk to him or her. This will burst the bubble of your fantasy, bring you back down to earth and reveal the beloved's flaws, alongside their virtues. It may also, possibly, set you on a path to a relationship.

Second, get to know yourself. Love is blind, because when obsessed by it you are blind to your real state of mind. It feels like an exquisite pleasure; the most noble feeling in the universe. But to everyone around you, you are merely deluded. Those who are infatuated neither know their beloved nor themselves.

Third, get out of this mad state. This is the most difficult thing but it is the first thing you must do. Hippothales hadn't managed it by the end of Plato's dialogue. Every time Socrates turned to him, he blushed again and shook his head. Even during the glorious rush of the madness, tell yourself to slow down. Eventually you will.

THE GREENER LIFE

25

'God Almighty first planted a garden.'

Francis Bacon

It is remarkable how frequently gardens are equated with the good life. Epicurus was an early philosopher to act on this connection. He called the philosophy school he set up in 306 BCE, 'the Garden'. It is not entirely clear whether he and his students actually did much gardening: someone can have disastrous green fingers and brilliant grey matter. Epicurus considered that the city, the place in which most philosophy had been done since Socrates, was antithetical to the tranquility he pursued through thought. The Garden was outside the city walls and so physically as well as imaginatively separated from the urban ways that he took to undermine the good life. As the later Epicurean writer, Philodemus of Gadara, put it: 'If a man were to undertake a systematic enquiry to find out what is most destructive of friendship and most productive of enmity, he would find it in the regime of the city.'

Marcus Aurelius complicated the picture slightly by insisting that the garden of nature was appealing because of its decay as well as its growth:

> The same is true of figs: it is when they are at their ripest that they burst open. In the case of very ripe olives, it is precisely their proximity to decay which adds to them a certain beauty ... Thus, as long as one has a feeling for and a deep understanding of Nature's processes, there is scarcely any of the things that occur as incidental by-products which will not present itself to one as pleasant, at least in some aspects.

Spinoza returns us to the high praise for gardens with his pantheism; the idea that there is no radical distinction between God and nature, meaning that nature is itself part of God. In other words, Spinoza rejected the biblical idea that God, in the lovely expression, walked through Eden 'in the cool of the day' because he reasoned God must be the good garden itself and you cannot walk through that which you are.

The pleasure garden, popular in the eighteenth and nineteenth centuries, manifested something of the good life envisaged by another group of philosophers, the Utilitarians. These parks were public amenities, containing amusements as well as landscape planting. I happen to live near to the site of one of the finest, the Vauxhall Pleasure Gardens. All that remains of it now is undulating scrubland, cast in shadow by the railway viaduct that carries trains to London's Waterloo Station. But it must have been a magnificent sight, as in this description from the 1830 edition of the *Edinburgh Encyclopædia*:

> The gardens' great attraction arises from their being splendidly illuminated at night with about 15,000 glass lamps. These being tastefully hung among the trees, which line the walks, produce an impression similar to that which is called up on reading some of the stories in the Arabian Nights Entertainments. On some occasions there have been upwards of 19,000 persons in them and this immense concourse, most of whom are well dressed, seen in connection with the illuminated walks, add not a little to the brilliant and astonishing effect of the whole scene.

The collective experience of the crowds who flocked to meander through them was thought to be morally beneficial. John Locke talked of 'inner civility' when describing such well-being; pleasure gardens were one place it could be felt.

Gardens are not only associated with versions of paradise in Western thought. There is a Chinese proverb: 'If you want to be happy for a lifetime, grow chrysanthemums.' The Koran conceives of heavenly bliss as life in a garden: 'This is the Paradise which the righteous have been promised: it is watered by running streams: eternal are its fruits and eternal are its shades.' Hence the lavishness of the Moorish *Generalife* gardens in Granada; they were created to mirror heaven. It is said that the Prophet would not enter the city of Damascus – whose 'gardens are thick-set with fruit trees of all kinds, kept fresh and verdant by the waters of Barrady' – because he feared he might confuse its beauty with the true beauty of paradise.

There is something else going on with gardens than simply that they are a refuge from the city or places cultivated for beauty. They remind people of the lost Eden to which the spirit aspires to return, as Francis Bacon noted: 'And indeed it is the purest of human pleasures. It is the greatest refreshment to the spirits of man; without which, buildings and palaces are but gross handiworks.'

For the more secularly minded, a garden perhaps echoes back to a pre-modern existence in which the world might have been an inter-locking realm of being, filled with cycles that both transcended and were impervious to human intervention. Unlike the modern urbanite who ignores the seasons in air-conditioned rooms and defies the night with electric light, gardeners are wise: they have stopped fighting against nature and determined to work with it. A glimpse of this good life, perhaps in a humble back garden or on a warmly shot television gardening programme, recalls what Max Weber called the 'enchanted garden.'

Gardens are therapeutic, partly because they are places in which time runs more slowly, year by year, not second by second, partly because they represent nature to us, which is both a free gift and an old ideal and also because they work on the unconscious. If Eden was a mythical garden, the Garden Centre is a shrine where people pur-chase the means of converting dreams into reality.

But be warned: before taking up the trowel, remember that gar-dens can also come to haunt their devotees. Very quickly, they demand more and more attention, for they never stand still. Shakespeare, in the figure of Hamlet, noticed how a suicidal feeling is like an 'unweeded garden, that grows to seed'. Eden was paradise but it was also the place of humanity's fall.

26

'Growth for the sake of growth is the philosophy of the cancer cell.'

Edward Abbey

The anxiety green issues cause governments is palpable. The science is clear enough and the economic case for tackling global warming is commanding. To take one figure: according to the Stern report, 1 per cent of Gross Domestic Product spent reducing the world's carbon output now would save a crash of up to 20 per cent over the next few decades. Yet still governments equivocate. It is not, for the most part, that they think nothing should be done. It is that they are unsure what they can get away with – partly in the sense of what is actually required to save the planet and more importantly in the sense of what citizens can stomach in terms of increased taxes or decreased choices. Thus, one of the key messages put about is that climate change can be tackled with only a minimal impact upon economic growth: the planet can be saved and it won't hurt that much either!

Economic growth. It is a shibboleth, because it is nothing short of the raison d'être of global capitalism. It is the relentless push to be more productive which few question. The thought is that with the material things increased wealth brings, who would want to live in a world that started to question the merits of economic growth?

This is the assumption that the environmental crisis is challenging. The force behind Edward Abbey's quote increasingly seems no longer misplaced but quite sensible. For all that, it is still radical. In developing economies, like China and India, the desirability of growth is obvious: to lift millions out of poverty – though if the planet continues to heat up, that success will be short-lived. But for those in the developed and already affluent West, it is a question worth asking.

Even before people began to feel they were being greedy or selfish for liking big cars and cheap flights, the growth imperative was making life for many feel like yet another desperate squeeze of the toothpaste when, in truth, the tube was long empty. Adam Smith wrote that the pleasures of wealth 'strike the imagination as something grand and beautiful and noble, of which the attainment is well worth all the toil and anxiety which we are so apt to bestow upon it'. He lived in the eighteenth century, during the infancy of modern capitalism. Now in its middle and perhaps old age, that toil is not so obviously worthwhile. Anxiety about the work-life balance, about how to be happy, about the damage being done to childhood – all have suggested that something is amiss in the unquestioning worship of economic growth.

It is possible that being tied to growth is a necessary evil; that nurturing greed is dismal in itself, though results in some good. At times it may feel like the punishment of Prometheus, having no end. But for making the world about as good as it can be, there simply seems to be no better system than free market economics. As long, that is, as free market economics can solve climate change.

A major problem for those who would like to live otherwise is that it is hard to resist the gospel of growth even if you want to. Like Christianity in a medieval monastery, it is the only ideology around. People perhaps sense it when they go to work: it is as if they have to hang their personal ethics at the door, with their coat, as they enter the office. The altruistic gene switches off, for they would never treat people so ruthlessly at home. This forced behaviour has been called the 'corrosion of character' by Richard Sennett.

Progressive managers would prefer their staff not to feel so schizoid. Enlightened ones try to make their organisations places in which the gulf between private kindness and professional harshness is narrowed. But it is hard. Business culture is utilitarian. It exists to please markets and markets reward growth. So, what the employee does is judged by what they deliver and what they have to do to deliver may differ from what they would like to do to be kind. A more ethical approach would nurture a culture that is not utilitarian but virtuous. Then, what you do would be judged by the kind of person it makes you; who you are would count for more than what you deliver. If that sounds like Alice in Wonderland commerce, that's probably because it is.

Having said that, some organisations have goals other than growth. Charles Handy mulls over cases in which more is not always better in his book *Myself and Other More Important Matters:*

> I sometimes suggest to business executives that if they were to ask a symphony orchestra what its growth plans were for the coming year, they might not speak of increasing the number of musicians or even the number of performances but would talk more of growing their repertoire and their reputation. Yes, more money would help but only as a means to achieve those ends. It is not different for other arts organisations or schools, better often when smaller.

To challenge the place of economic growth in the modern way of life would be, therefore, nothing less than a paradigm change. Think of the difference between the goals of today's economics and those of pre-capitalist times. Then, the goal was to supply people with their basic needs: water, bread and clothing were valuable; anything else was a luxury. Today luxuries have become basics: a household is poor if it is without a car, a television and a washing machine; water, bread and clothing have taken on the status of utilities.

If it is hard to imagine what life was like before shopping made consumption a leisure activity, it is harder to imagine what life might be like without shopping as a leisure activity. Put like that, it sounds ghastly! But perhaps Charles Handy's discussion about the symphony orchestra conveys a more appealing possibility. It would be one in which money was not the only measure of growth but where your growth as a human being counted too. Growth could mean not just spending-power but also reputation. And inasmuch as economic growth was still desirable, it would be a means clearly distinguished from other, richer ends.

Governments cannot effect that change. If they tried they would become totalitarian. The hope is that individuals, to a degree, can.

27

'A good piece of technology dreams of the day when it will be replaced by a newer piece of technology.'

Douglas Coupland

What have uranium-235, people and washing machines got in common? They all have built-in obsolescence.

Being radioactive, uranium-235 decays. Though it has a half-life counted in billions of years, slowly but surely it disappears, morphing into thorium-231.

Being mortal, people decline. They have a full life of something over three score years and ten. So slowly but surely they die, morphing into dust.

Being technology, washing machines deteriorate. They have an estimated life of approximately twenty years. Not quite so slowly but equally as surely, they spin, then stutter and finally stop, morphing into scrap metal.

Except that washing machines don't usually live out the whole of their allotted time. They are often dumped before they deteriorate. Why? Their obsolescence differs in nature from that of uranium-235 and people. It is what is known in the trade as 'planned obsolescence'.

Planned obsolescence is when a product is designed to become outmoded before it stops working. Commercially, this keeps markets active. Obsolescence can be planned in two ways: sometimes, all that is required is to rely on the fact that technology falls in price and increases in power. Games consoles, MPEG players and PCs are obvious cases in point: in Coupland's words, they are good pieces of technology because they are created obsolete, the technology having moved on by the time they reach the market.

At other times, technology's dream of being replaced requires human assistance to be fulfilled. Washing machines are like this, since the increase in power and fall in price of your front- or top-loader is not quick enough to sustain the required levels of commercial dynamism – for which read, the rapid purchase of new models. Instead, manufacturers encourage consumers to think their old machine is obsolete. They build washer-dryers, add more programmes or include ecologically friendly features. More recently, the Dyson company introduced the two-cylinder machine: how redundant did all your white goods look then?! Now you can buy machines with a WiFi connection that links to a 'domotic network' so you can check the progress of your wash on a website (that's with two 'o's: there is nothing common about this piece of kit).

Planned obsolescence becomes somewhat suspect in an age of environmental concerns. It encourages us to buy energy-hungry novelties and throw out old ones that did perfectly well. But, say, the manufacturers: don't blame us, for planned obsolescence is a subtle feature of technology itself. The story they tell is that technology is the appliance of science. Scientists discover the laws of nature which technologists then put to good use. The assumption is of the inevitable progress of technology, driven by the inevitable progress of science. Similarly, obsolescence is inevitable in the devices progress produces.

However, this understanding of the process is inadequate according to others who have closely studied exactly how new technologies emerge. They notice two things: first, that technology progresses in discrete steps, rather than advancing continuously. All sorts of technologies are developed but the market standardises only around the one that wins the race to be adopted: whichever novelty catches on is sold as the next generation of technology. It need not be the best advance (remember Betamax video recorders) or even an advance at all: think of fax machines, which continue to appear as new models – doubling up as scanners or printers – although the Internet clearly renders them redundant. In other words, obsolescence is not, strictly speaking, a feature of technology but a feature of the human desire for novelty.

The second thing that has been noticed is even more profound. Only infrequently, at times of paradigm change, is a new technology related to the discovery of a new law of nature. Even then, it is usually technology that leads: the technology emerges first and the laws of nature come later. Faraday built the first electric motor by experimenting with wire, mercury and magnets; only later did Maxwell articulate the fundamental equations of electromagnetism, his law of nature.

This has led a few philosophers, like Martin Heidegger, to conclude that the so-called laws of nature are actually only abstracted technology and that technology is not the application of those laws but the manipulation of nature for human ends.

The truth of the matter is probably somewhere in between. But this highlights the point that we need not be led by technology. The obsolescence of the washing machine is artificial. Technology can be built to suit needs, as opposed to needs being created to suit the death wish of technology.

28

'Nature favours those organisms which leave the environment in better shape for their progeny to survive.'

James Lovelock

By chance, I found myself sitting next to a climate change expert. Our paths crossed at an awards ceremony. We would be neighbours for the duration of the meal. I must seize my chance, I thought and ask all I wanted to know about climate change but had never before been in a position directly to ask.

My expert was Dr Dave Reay, of Edinburgh University. Ocean science is his specialism but he has considered the wider issues in his book, *Climate Change Begins at Home*, which was featured on no less than the BBC TV *Climate Chaos* series, with David Attenborough.

I had three questions. First, does the science confirm that dangerous climate change is occurring? I have always tended to think it does. But then you read debates between passionate and apparently equally well-informed protagonists – both of whom seem to have at least a bit of an axe to grind – and it is hard to work out who is right. I suspect these debates will continue for some time yet: science always comes with an uncertainty that vested interests can exploit.

Dr Reay's answer was straightforward: yes, it is occurring. The arguments that are usually put about to undermine the evidence are bogus. One is medieval warming, the fact that there was warming in Europe in the medieval period that did no long-term damage. It did happen but it was a local phenomenon. But, continued Dr Reay, what is happening now is dangerous because it is global and on a completely different scale. If you want the truth, he said, see Al Gore's movie *An Inconvenient Truth*.

My second question was whether the problem is solvable? I am equivocal on this. I know that there is technology to remove carbon, save energy and so on but the political and social will that is necessary to back the technology is almost unthinkably massive. I also suspect that going for a global, Kyoto-agreement-style solution, is to aim too high and will take too long. This seems doubly so when you link it to the latest trends in international commerce: globalisation appears to be breaking down, shown by bilateral deals between China and Africa, American protectionism, European regionalism and the persistent failure of world trade talks. Piecemeal regional deals and local initiatives, powered by industries or governments, are perhaps more likely to bring about the changes necessary – though they must spread widely, of course. This underlines the social imperative required to change behaviour that, already, people are resisting as 'nanny-stateism', when encouraged by governments. Businesses are adept at avoiding regulations by locating their carbon-intense activities in parts of the world less likely to take climate change seriously. On top of this, when has social change in the past ever spread around the planet in a matter of years, as is needed now?

Dr Reay said that the technological means to reduce carbon dioxide by the 60 per cent necessary does exist. But, he agreed, the political and social issues are huge. However, he was more optimistic now than he has been in the past. The subject has risen up the agenda extraordinarily rapidly.

My third question was more direct: does he fly? I do and I am conscious it is the single biggest contribution to my 'carbon footprint'. I take a slight comfort from the fact that at the moment flying contributes only 3 per cent of the UK's output, though this figure is rising. To put the question a different way, does he think the climate change threat is a moral imperative that should prompt significant, personally costly changes in what we do?

He said he does not fly. Not that he will never fly again but that on a case by case basis, he just hasn't seen the moral justification to fly in recent years. Not flying has probably had a negative effect on his career, since he has missed foreign academic conferences: not flying is costly for him but the moral case for not doing so demands it. As to the 3 per cent, he said that the figure is based on old science. Aircraft outputs are rising very rapidly and will contribute a carbon dioxide level measured in the tens of per cent in a decade and, at current rates, will continue to rise quickly.

Dr Reay is a moderate man, in manner and argument: I imagine he is not given to extreme positions and yet, he is in no doubt about the seriousness of climate change. It was encouraging to talk to him, because he is optimistic and that optimism is growing. Though I have to say that although I came away from our conversation settled about the science I was unsure about its ramifications – in terms both of the impact at the level of personal behaviour and decisions, and about whether the world is capable of the political and social change required.

THE EXAMINED LIFE

29

'For our discussion is about no ordinary matter but on the right way to conduct our lives.'

Plato

In his short book, *Morality*, the late Bernard Williams, one of the United Kingdom's most eminent philosophers, remarked: 'The number of great books on the subject (as opposed to books involved in one way or another in morality) can be literally counted on the fingers of one hand.'

A teasing comment: which does he think the great books are and are there actually only five or fewer? Another philosopher, Adrian Moore, had the presence of mind to ask Professor Williams when he had the chance. It turns out that the ones Williams was thinking of were:

1. Plato's complete dialogues – one book if you wrap them up together.
2. Aristotle's *Nicomachean Ethics*.
3. David Hume's *Second Enquiry Concerning the Principles of Morals*.
4. Immanuel Kant's *Foundations of the Metaphysics of Morals*.
5. Nietzsche's complete works – again, if you bundle them.

Given that Williams was right, is it possible to generate, from these heavyweight books, a synthesis of high-level insights about how we are to live?

Plato begins with the assumption that we live for happiness: we do not want to live like animals but to live good lives, as befits being human. But notice: he has already made a move that is not obvious. He started with happiness and immediately equated that with virtuousness. His case is that happiness requires more than just luck, like the good fortune to be healthy and wealthy. There is a skill in living well that in turn requires a practical intelligence manifest in the exercise of the virtues. This does not come naturally. And so the question of how we are to live comes down to how you can transform your way of life so that virtuousness comes to dominate. How that transformation may be brought about is the ethical theme that runs through his dialogues.

Aristotle agrees with Plato on the intimacy between happiness and virtuousness. However, there is something less austere about his view of what it takes. Given certain minimal requirements, like being healthy and wealthy enough, a good moral life – by which he means a successful, flourishing life – begins by emulating role models. Then, in a process of critical engagement with these lives, an individual can become more reflective about their own life and develop the excellences that come most naturally to them. Someone engaged in public or civic life, for example, will excel in virtues such as courage, generosity and fair-mindedness; someone engaged in a more philosophical life, as was Aristotle, will excel in virtues such as reason, perseverance and contemplation. If someone has the capacity to pursue both, Aristotle's thought is that the intellectual life is the better choice. There is something divine in human beings, he argued, supremely shown in the intellectual life, so that must be the best possible life in us.

In his *Enquiry*, David Hume asks a pragmatic question: how do we make moral decisions? He concludes that most decisions are thought moral because they increase the public good. It might be concluded from this that people mostly act according to self-interest – that is, not especially morally. However, Hume thought that people have a keen sense of sympathy for others, a characteristic shown, for example, in the ability to empathise. Moreover, we have to rely on our sympathy more than our reason, since reason is too blunt a tool to hone most of the decisions we make in life. This has a most beneficial outcome: it is as if human beings are born with the fortunate propensity to act altruistically in spite of ourselves. So how are we to live? By deepening our sense of others.

Immanuel Kant reacts against Hume's so-called sentimentalism (meaning of the senses, rather than sentimental about human beings).

It offended him by suggesting that morality comes from within, rather than from a rational authority external to us. He thought this a minimal requirement for any decent moral system, not least in an age when God, as arbiter, was quickly disappearing. But if not God, then what could guarantee morality? His response was the categorical imperative: the idea that any individual should act as they would want anyone else to act. This leads to universal laws that everyone will obey everywhere – none of that soft sentimental stuff. However, there is one element of morality that Hume and Kant would share. People should be treated as ends in themselves, not means to some other end. For Kant, we live by doing what reason judges right.

Nietzsche is the black sheep in this disparate family of mega-moralists. The other four don't agree but Nietzsche wants to ditch the whole debate. He is not easily summed up: he probably should not be summarised, for to try to distil a simple moral theme from his writings would be to fall foul of one of his main critiques of morality: too often, it ceases to be an art aimed at enlarging an individual's life and becomes a convention aimed at containing it. Christianity is the quintessential case in point: according to Nietzsche, it answers the question of how to live with the slavish imperative to follow a rule-book. Nietzsche is also a pessimist, not because he suffered from black moods but because he thought the myth of human progress – moral or material – to be deluded. In a way, his answer to the question of how to live is to develop a way of life that shakes you free of this myth, to be able to embrace the radical uncertainties of the human condition.

These five authors are morality's greats yet there is no synthesis to be generated from their theses and antitheses, bar perhaps one insight. If you want to know how to live, you must do it – live, that is. For what is morality without acting and acting skilfully, at that.

30

'You must be the change you wish to see in the world.'

Gandhi

The horrors of the war in Iraq and its neocon inception – which in part takes a lead from the philosophy of Leo Strauss and the use of force to export democracy – is a chilling reminder that philosophers do political programmes at their peril. Grand theories are incapable of accounting for the countless forces that forge the history of humankind. If you insist on implementing them as a philosophical programme, you end up brutally shaping the world to them, not they to the world. Leninism, Trotskyism and Stalinism are the watchwords; the ghastly manifestations of the philosophical programme of Communism. And there are others.

Ask Plato, who tried to put his philosophy to use in Syracuse and failed to moderate the tyrant Dionysius the Younger. Or Aristotle, who clearly had very little impact on the megalomania of Alexander the Great. Cicero had great philosophical style but tried to conceal his political lack of substance, at least according to Montaigne: the Roman Republic stepped closer to collapse on Cicero's watch. Seneca? He was the tutor of Nero! Perhaps Marcus Aurelius is the exception to the rule – except that many of his *Meditations* read as a withdrawal from the brutalities he meted out as emperor.

Little wonder that many ancient philosophers advocated taking no part in politics at all – like Heraclitus, who preferred playing with his children to playing politics; Epicurus, who thought nothing more undermining of happiness; and Diogenes who when visited by

Alexander and asked what the ruler of the world could do for him, replied: 'Get out of my light.'

I once heard the British Conservative MP Oliver Letwin, who has a PhD in philosophy, speaking about the role of philosophy in politics. He was cautious, saying it had only a secondary part to play, inasmuch as philosophers have a habit of trying to think clearly. This sensibility is useful in politics.

There are ethical principles that philosophy can highlight. Parties of the right have often looked to Edmund Burke in support of the principle of conservatism: 'Good order is the foundation of all good things,' he wrote, though he added, 'A state without the means of some change is without the means of its conservation.' The parties of the left retain their socialism, to the extent that they adhere to the principle that the natural priorities of free markets must be steered away from the ends of the rich and towards the needs of the poor. John Stuart Mill inspired the modern definition of liberty that all democracies follow: 'The liberty of the individual must be thus far limited; he must not make himself a nuisance to other people.'

More particularly, if Bush and Blair had paid more attention to the Just War theory, first conceived by the medieval philosopher Thomas Aquinas, they might have avoided the bloody mess of Iraq. This theory judges their war to be unjust because it was not possible to achieve the good ends they had in mind by the appalling means they undertook – whether those good ends were the removal of Saddam, the removal of WMD, the sowing of democracy or some combination of the three. Even without hindsight, it should have been ruled out on the means necessary alone.

There are also ethical goals that philosophers can enrich in political discourse, like the pursuit of happiness. Though remember: Socrates, who was a distinguished soldier in his prime and not averse to getting his hands dirty, took his later calling as a philosopher to be primarily prophetic. He niggled at the politicians of his day, because he was disillusioned with them; he asks those who think that something must be done – and rush to stand for office in order to do it – whether they seek power without really thinking through what they will do should they gain it.

The 'consumer politics' of our day seems particularly vulnerable to this critique. In the intense struggle to win elections – and combat negative campaigning, a personality-obsessed media and the indifference of voters – politicians rarely have time to ponder what to do with power. I once helped run a political think-tank and invited leading politicians to deliver thoughtful papers on ethical issues in public life. They always let us down, in their content, because they did not have the time to put in the thought.

Which brings us back to Gandhi. A student of Hindu philosophy, he lived simply, fasted often, preached non-violence and insisted on wearing his trademark loincloth even before heads of state. The cynic would say that this was merely politically canny because it was disarming. But it stresses a philosophical principle that must be at the heart of any politics of change. His way of life came before his politics; he worked on himself before his plan for revolution. Unlike almost every other political leader you could name, he was a master of his own vices: his politics did not serve to nourish or incite them, in glory or good intentions; it starved and quelled them.

You must be the change you wish to see in the world.

31

'Seize the day!'

Horace

One of my earliest memories has to do with time. I was about five or six years old, the age at which children learn to read clocks. I do not remember mastering the skill itself – making the leap from observing that 'the big hand is on the six and the little hand is in between the four and five', to seeing, instantaneously, the hands showing half past four. No. What sticks in my mind was a revelation: time passes. A second has duration. This is what an hour feels like (at that age, interminably long).

This diachronic wonder came with a sense both of challenge and panic, for if time passes, 'spiteful minutes steal away', as Horace puts it in his ode from which his famous aphorism comes. This is why the wheels of a clock rotate with unremitting resolution; their brass teeth never falter as they count the seconds. They mirror the infinite force with which time itself proceeds. And it cannot be stopped! I remember trying to hold on to time. I envisaged it as a long, taut piece of fabric that if I could grip I could stretch, lengthening its seconds. The trouble was that I could glimpse the fabric only in my peripheral vision and when I turned to look at it head on, it had vanished. The instant I needed time to dwell on was gone before I could appreciate its passing.

The elusive quality of time and its sovereignty in conscious life is implicit in the phrase 'telling the time'. It sounds like 'reading the runes', as if time has to be told like a story or interpreted like a text. Perhaps this nod to the mysteriousness of time is not surprising, given the variety of experiences of it one can have even in the course of a single day.

Someone will awake from sleep with no sense of the hours that have passed. They will rush to work, conscious of every minute. At work, time comes in two large chunks: before lunch and after lunch. The former may feel shorter than the latter, though they are both about four hours long. In the evening, in front of the television, they are anesthetised to time. Or if the evening is spent with friends, conversation and wine, it may approach something close to bliss, though that too will disappear, so that the next day they cannot remember quite what was said or happened.

Time's resistance to being pinned down escapes even the world's most accurate chronometers. They can measure it to within 0.000000001 seconds per day but are inaccurate because an identical clock orbiting the Earth, would show a different time upon returning to terra firma. Which clock is right? Einstein showed that the answer is both and neither.

For ancient philosophers, time was a crucial concern. They too grappled with its chicanery. Take a period of time, Zeno said. It can be divided into two periods of equal duration. These two can be halved again. And again. And again, until one has an infinity of periods of time emerging out of the original single whole. The paradox is how an infinite amount of time can fit into a period of specific duration. Mathematically speaking, what Zeno had identified was a conundrum of infinity. Existentially speaking, his thought experiment beautifully dissects time, showing how it can be fleeting in one instance and full in another.

This leads to another aspect of the ancient philosopher's concern with time. It had to do with nothing less than how to live a good life. The nub of the problem is how to live in the present – how to seize the day, in Horace's expression. They realised that the challenge is to dwell neither on the past, something that comes very easily because it is known and so tangible in memories; nor on the future, that also comes easily, because it can be filled with hopes or anxieties. The challenge is to dwell in the present, which is hard to do, because it is neither the past nor the future.

The ancient philosophers had another insight to help people: it is a mistake to think of the present as the point at which the past and the future meet. This is a natural thing to do; the arrow of time feels like the movement from yesterday into tomorrow. However, this sensibility denies the present autonomy. It is, in effect, forced to be either the end of the past or the beginning of the future, with the result that it is not now.

How else might time and the present in particular be experienced? As attention. We are living now and not in the past or the future. The present therefore enjoys a 'thickness' that the past has lost and the future is yet to realise. This thickness can be attended to: the way to live is not diachronically but synchronically, within contemporary thoughts and actions. To use the metaphor of my childhood, the trick is to release the fabric of the present from the grip of the two opposing forces.

The Stoics and the Epicureans, who disagreed on much, agreed on this matter. The exercises they recommended to cultivate the present discouraged the tendency to limit it by forcing it in between the past and the future. The Stoic Marcus Aurelius counselled himself mentally to discard anything that disturbed him from his past and to refuse to contemplate anything that worried him about the future:

> If you can separate from yourself the future and the past and apply yourself exclusively to living the life that you are living – that is to say, the present – you can live the time that remains to you until your death in calm, benevolence and serenity.

The Epicureans strove to inculcate the same synchronousness, by drawing attention to a truth about pleasure: that the intensity of any pleasure (or for that matter pain) is time independent. 'Finite time and infinite time bring us the same pleasure, if we measure its limits by reason,' Epicurus wrote – arguing that a pleasure promised even indefinitely into the future does not increase our appreciation, since our capacity to enjoy it is limited to our capacity to enjoy it now.

It is hard to fault their logic but in reality the present moment is not grasped so straightforwardly. Many might prefer 'to take no thought for the morrow,' as the Gospel of Matthew puts it yet cannot help but worry none the less. It might seem right that pleasure is time-independent but then is not the promise of indefinite pleasure an added pleasure in itself?

Worse, much of modern life actively discourages us from living in the here and now. In the same way that shares on a stock market are priced according to their future returns, not current value, so life tends to be thought of according to its potential. Preoccupations from credit-ratings and health insurance to pensions and house prices work to drive our attention forward. Richard Sennett has argued that an individual's worth is oriented towards the future too, because companies no longer hire someone for what they can do now but for the extent to which they can be trained to face the, as yet unknown, challenges of tomorrow. People even consume prospectively, buying a high-powered computer 'just in case' the extra processor speed is needed; buying a high-powered car 'just in case' the opportunity arises to push the accelerator to the floor. And who cannot but help feel that the person who does not want the fast car – or whatever it is with which this Janus obsession tempts you – is missing something from life? It is almost impossible to believe that someone who did separate themselves from the past and the future would 'have everything,' as Seneca put it.

It seems that the promise of the future and nostalgia for the past are written into the stressed fabric of modern lives (the two go together because the complexities of the future seek consolation in the simplicities of the past). *Carpe diem*? Even if someone wanted to, it is far from clear they could.

If radical expunging is not a practical option, then perhaps attending to the present can be practised by a radical examination of what comes more easily: petty thoughts. They fill the present. Except perhaps when we are asleep or on holiday or making love, they are the present. Marcus Aurelius recognised this and turned his trivial thoughts into his *Meditations*. (This is partially why they don't contain many big political thoughts, for all that he was emperor.) His aim was, first, to notice them and, then, to transcend them, in universal maxims that put them into perspective. 'Withdraw into yourself,' he wrote, perhaps at worrying news of revolting barbarian hordes. 'Do away with all fancies,' he thought, maybe because peacock tongue and dormice were on the menu again.

The advantage of attending to petty thoughts is twofold. First, they exist in the present and so exercise the practice of the present. And second, as they are discarded, they are objectified, which again reinforces the sense of the present.

It requires effort, for at first and for some time, the practice of the present must be consciously sustained second by second by second. 'How easy it is to find oneself, right away, in a state of perfect peace of mind,' the philosopher-emperor also wrote. He could be intimating that practice makes perfect.

32

"'Tis not contrary to reason to prefer the destruction of the whole world to the scratching of my finger.'

David Hume

You take a trip to the coast with two friends. One is an old friend and probably your closest. One is a new friend, though the relationship holds great promise, since together you are working on an idea that you feel passionate about and sense could be very lucrative to boot.

After a leisurely lunch, the sun feels hot and the sea is sparkling. So you decide to enjoy the water. All three of you take the plunge and swim out. Then disaster strikes: both your friends are attacked by severe cramps. They become distressed and, heads disappearing now for longer and longer periods in between breaths, they start to drown. You can only save one? Who should it be?

Welcome to the world of thought experiments. Such a scenario might be proposed as a way to ponder the moral imperatives of friendship. Should shared history count for more than future hopes? Should emotional connection outweigh the realisation of a personal passion? And what about the financial element: is that what really lies behind the new friendship and will it now end an old one horribly?

Thought experiments are the staple of a certain kind of moral philosophy. If a woman, heavily pregnant, faces a life-threatening illness which means she can lose the baby and live or save the baby and die, which course of action is right? If telling a lie would save a life, should you tell the lie? These might be relatively easy questions to address. So how about this: if a passenger plane carrying three hundred people is about to crash into a skyscraper housing the same number, should you shoot the plane out of the air? Or, if shopping at a local supermarket supports jobs in developing countries but also supports the poor wages of those workers, should you shop at the local supermarket? As the situations become more mundane, the process of deciding becomes more frustrating. Do you let the kids watch rubbish on the TV, to give yourself a break; or do you entertain the kids yourself, to give them constructive stimulation? Should a man hold the door open for a woman and let her go through first – or is this demeaning for the woman and patronising of the man? Wars have been fought over less.

There is a flaw in such an approach to ethics: it is not really ethics at all. The scenarios may or may not be plausible. But the question forced by the scenario is not one that is likely ever to be asked with the expectation that the answer would then inform what should be done.

Take the ones that deal with emergency situations of life and death. These are not ethical questions, because in such situations the question is not what is it right to do. In fact, you probably wouldn't ask a question at all. If I was yards from the beach and my friends were drowning, I would not decide whether to save my old or new friend, I would act on impulse. Afterwards, I would have to live with what I did but not with what I decided. For, in the panic of the moment, I decided nothing. In reality, all eventualities would be tragic. Luck would probably have more of a role in settling who survived.

Consider the thought experiments that posit extreme situations, where there might be time to make a partial decision, such as whether or not to shoot the plane out of the sky. Yet again, the thought process is present only in the thought experiment, not in real life. In the passenger plane case, the 'decision' would actually have been taken long before, when the soldier pressing the button, the officer issuing the command and the politician taking responsibility had decided that they would follow the policy that had been set months, possibly years ago. The soldier, the officer and the politician might well sense the horror of what was happening. We hope they would, for it would keep them human – and prevent them falling foul of what Hannah Arendt famously called the 'banality of evil'. But the value of that feeling is also its tragedy; it reflects the fact that there and then, there is no moral choice to be made, only an order to follow.

The decision about whether the women or her child should survive is similar, inasmuch as it would be the woman who would live because it is her that the doctors had implicitly committed to saving when she first went to them. They would feel terrible and might rationalise the 'decision' in response. But that would be a way of coping with what is, rationally speaking, more or less undecidable.

Finally, consider the thought experiments that are mundane. There is no emergency here, so again it might be supposed that someone could reason about the immediate situation and then act on what they decided. And yet to behave in this way would only lead to ethical constipation, not action. The man who wonders whether or not to hold the door open on the basis of a patriarchal calculation is likely to look more foolish through indecision, than through holding it or not. Certainly, a misogynist upbringing might be challenged by thinking about feminism, as an uncertain liberal temperament might be even more confused by it. But this is something that would have to happen in another time and place, not as the door was swinging.

Similarly, there is no real decision about supermarket shopping and its ambivalent benefits at the moment when I need to stock up with mangetout and milk. I am conscious of the dilemma and that is good, because it keeps my human sympathies alive. But if I were to stop shopping at supermarkets, it would be the result of a growing discomfort with market forces and a particular perception of them that grew over time. The moral content of any potential decision to shop elsewhere would be found in a discussion of why I became suspicious of this aspect of the capitalist system, what my new choice hopes to achieve and whether it is about other things, such as the assuaging of guilt.

Ethics, when posited as rational, piecemeal decisions is barely ethics at all. In the heat of the moment, reason fails us. As David Hume wittily expressed it: ''Tis not contrary to reason to prefer the destruction of the whole world to the scratching of my finger.' The point is that the real task of ethics must embrace life in the round, for ethics is nothing if it is not the great project of how to live. Unless or until we become computers and act only after myriad impersonal calculations, that is not how we should think that we live either. Ethics is the whole of life; to think ethically is a way of life.

33

'The unexamined life is not worth living.'

Socrates

Socratic dialogue is in fashion. It is appealed to in a variety of contexts but is any of it genuine?

A certain kind of self-helper likes the idea of Socratic dialogue. Its attraction is the thought that people can be encouraged to form their own opinions about things by being asked searching questions: it is self-help because drawn out, rather than forced in. However, the danger is that such self-help encourages the insidious doctrine that any opinion is as good as any other, the only criterion for truth being that it is your own. That is, it nurtures a relativism of the kind peddled by the Sophists – whom Socrates loathed.

Socratic dialogue is also referred to in contexts such as the philosophy programmes suggested for schools. The attraction here is that it develops a way of thinking clearly, by being inquisitive about the world and asking questions. The better the questions, the better the Socratic-style thought. There is something in this but it risks missing an important element in Socrates' philosophy; that the aim of thinking clearly was not thought for its own sake but was as a precursor to changing yourself. The person who thinks clearly takes the first step in freeing themselves of delusion. The danger is that if thinking clearly is presented as a kind of wisdom in itself it may increase the delusion, not dissolve it.

The real task was captured in Plato's Socratic dialogues: it is a way of talking that explores wisdom as being not so much about what you know as being about how well you understanding the limits of what you know.

The danger of forgetting this is that the budding philosopher becomes either fatalistically pessimistic – believing that thought dissolves in relativism; or fatally optimistic – believing that reason can triumph not by asking good questions but by answering them.

This is why Socrates was famously ironic. He used irony in a number of ways. Didactically, like a good teacher, he identified with those with whom he talked, although he could be pretty sure of what they would say and how he would reply. But his irony more fundamentally reflected the fact that the philosopher – the lover of wisdom – loves what they, at best, never quite and at worst, never remotely, have. For irony, read sanity.

34

'A person's character is their fate.'

Heraclitus

For the first twenty years of his life, John Stuart Mill thought he understood the key to its success. He was committed to his godfather Jeremy Bentham's goal of working for the greatest happiness of the greatest number. To this end, he regarded himself as a social and political reformer through and through and it brought tremendous satisfaction. Powerful influences, notably his father, who regarded Bentham as a 'utilitarian messiah', had formed his character for this work. At the age of three he was reading Greek. He first seriously engaged with Bentham's writings in his early teens, noting, in passing, that he did so in French translation. It was a formative moment. Before, he only had scattered learnings, with no direction. Now he felt he had organised opinions, which added up to a quasi-religious purpose of life. What is humbling about his analysis of this precociousness, laid out in his *Autobiography*, is that he thought he was unexceptionally gifted and called his childhood happy, something not recorded by many other nineteenth-century autobiographers.

Then, at the age of twenty, he hit a wall of depression. It was as if his character, intellectually as deep as the ocean, was too narrow to allow him to pass into adulthood. He writes that if he had relentlessly pursued the direction of his life set by his youthful education, as if that were his fate, he would not have been open to the 'important transformation' in his character that his 'dull state of nerves' precipitated. As it was, it led him to ask a question. He could not have entertained a riskier one, for to allow it to surface in his mind was to challenge his sense of himself to the core: 'Suppose that all your objects in life were realised,' he asked. 'That all the changes in institutions and opinions which you are looking forward to could be completely effected at this very instant: would this be a great joy and happiness to you?'

His depression arouse because, at twenty, 'an irrepressible self-consciousness distinctly answered, "No!"'

What now would he live for? He turned to his books. There seemed to be nothing worthwhile in them. He examined his love of humankind. It had run dry. He turned to his philosophy of life. But it now seemed superficial and crude. He realised that his education – his character – had been based merely upon associations. That which was beneficial to the greatest number, he had trained himself to find pleasurable; that which was hurtful, painful. In particular, a religion of utilitarianism increasingly seemed inhuman to him, lacking in feeling and virtue. Albert Einstein thought similarly: 'To make a goal of comfort or happiness has never appealed to me; a system of ethics built on this basis would be sufficient only for a herd of cattle.' Why? It pursued pleasure but not passion. Months of melancholy haunted Mill, with the thought that there was 'no power in nature sufficient to begin the formation of my character anew'.

Habit drove him on. He worked without hope and composed without spirit. So determining of his future did the straitjacket of his analytical character feel, that he thought it would lead him to suicide within a year. Then, one day, he read Jean-François Marmontel, the French encyclopædist's account of the death of his father. Quite by surprise, it moved him to tears. The catharsis was like a ray of light through dusty gloom. Though not easy, a path back to enjoyment began to appear. 'I was no longer hopeless: I was not a stock or a stone. I had still, it seemed, some of the material out of which all worth of character and all capacity for happiness, are made.'

His character was transformed in two ways in particular. First, he adopted a different theory of life. No longer would happiness be its aim, though happiness is what everyone hopes for. Rather, he would focus on others or excellence or something else that was worthwhile in itself. Happiness, he thought, would come 'by the way': question your purpose in life, not your happiness, for that will thwart it. Second, Mill realised he must cultivate his feelings over and against the 'reasoning machine' of utilitarian calculus. He had developed a tremendous appreciation of music in his childhood, it giving 'a glow and a fervour' to his most elevated feelings, though he now feared that

familiarity might exhaust his enthusiasm for it. Now he discovered a
new source of meaning in poetry. It worked on his imagination and
allowed him to see life in its whole as well as in its parts. With the formation of a new character, Mill was released from his old fate.

Mill was lucky. He was young enough, resourceful enough and
strong enough to reform his character. Many feel they are not, be that
because of some fear or of a perceived lack of freedom. They imagine,
to recall another line of Heraclitus, that they are like a fly caught in a
web. Whenever they try to move in a new direction, character traits as
strong as steel hold them back. They worry what others might say or
about the risks they should take. They feel unfree because of debts or
dependants. Oh that they could be a spider to their hesitancies, able to
walk over the web, wrap worries in silk and cut them out of their lives!

To be stuck in a rut is to be trapped by life. However, do not forget how
profoundly Mill's character had been shaped. It had been fixed in childhood and contrary to today's received wisdom, was not actually set in
stone. The double transformation it underwent suggests two elements to
address should you wish to escape what otherwise appears like fate.

Consider first his new theory of life. The move to an indirect goal
of happiness was not just an excellent new insight about life in general.
It represented a subtle realignment of the narrative of his life in particular. What Mill achieved was not a rejection of his father's utilitarian convictions *tout à fait*, like a baby throwing the rattle out of the
pram. Rather, it reworked what he had received, to take him clearly in
a new direction. The lesson is this: if character is fate, 'charactercide'
is fatal. Zombies have no character. The trick is to question the past in
order to integrate it into the present, in pursuit of a different future.

Changing your story like this is only one part: the mental part. The
other affects the heart. If Mill's story is anything to go by, it may be
that the heart can only be changed precipitously – with a breakdown.
However, like tears, a breakdown is not necessarily all bad. It is surely
no coincidence that within three years of his recovery, Mill met the
person with whom he was to share the most valuable friendship of his
life. In 1830, he met Harriet Taylor and his tribute to their friendship
is surely one of the most moving ever written:

> I soon perceived that she possessed in combination, the qualities
> which in all other persons whom I had known I had been only too
> happy to find singly ... Alike in the highest regions of speculation and

in the smallest practical concerns of daily life, her mind was the same perfect instrument, piercing to the very heart and marrow of the matter; always seizing the essential principle ... Her intellectual gifts did but minister to a moral character at once the noblest and the best balanced which I ever met with in life ... To be admitted into any degree of mental intercourse with a being of these qualities, could not but have a most beneficial influence on my development; though the effect was only gradual and many years elapsed before her mental progress and mine went forward in the complete companionship they at last attained. The benefit I received was far greater than any which I could hope to give ... What I owe, even intellectually, to her, is, in its detail, almost infinite; of its general character, a few words will give some, though a very imperfect, idea.

His renewed character had become open to others. His new-found feeling realised that he needed another if he was to be anyone. He had arrived at a different understanding of success in life.

35

'"Know thyself?" If I knew myself, I'd run away.'

Goethe

To my mind, *The Neverending Story* by Michael Ende is better than *The Chronicles of Narnia* by C. S. Lewis – and not just because *The Neverending Story* inspired a super-smooth pop song, by Limahl, for its film version. Both feature fantasy lands in which child heroes fall into adventures that expose them to the complexities of adult life. Both can be sentimental, as well as serious. But where Ende's book wins, for me, is in its greater psychological richness.

This reaches a peak at the moment when the young warrior, Atreyu, faces the challenge of looking into the Magic Mirror Gate. Its magic lies in its capacity to reflect back an image of him as he is in himself: to look at this mirror is to look your true self in the face. Another character, Falcor, thinks this cannot be too hard but he does not realise that most people are strangers to themselves. That, says the wise sage Engywook, is what everyone overlooks, for the truth of yourself is often brutal: the kind are exposed as cruel; the brave as cowards. 'Confronted by their true selves, most men run away, screaming,' Engywook says ominously.

Goethe understood the fear. Recalling the injunction to 'Know thyself!' that was written above the entrance to the temple of the oracle at Delphi, he thought that he would turn on his heels and flee. He was thinking of Socrates, who famously adopted the phrase as his motto. Originally it meant: remember who you are before you enter this holy place – that is, not a god. Socrates took it not only to be a warning but also a quest. He reasoned that if we are less than gods, we are also more than animals; we might not have divine wisdom but we do have more understanding than the ignorant beasts. In particular, we can become conscious of the limits of our knowledge, of the world around us and of ourselves. This is the challenge: how can we, as humans – as 'in between' creatures – bring light to the darkness of the things that are hidden from us?

Philosophy was his answer. It consisted of two key parts. One part was what we would recognise as philosophy today, the use of reason to ask questions, such as why do we think what we think and how should we live. The value of such reasoning, for Socrates, was not so much that it establishes irrefutable truths, like a mathematical proof but rather that he thought it could be used to clarify the points at which our understanding reaches its limits, the boundaries of thought, when the light dims and intellectual darkness encroaches. This is the preliminary exercise in knowing yourself and it leads to the second part: developing ways of living that take care of this vulnerable, limited self. As Socrates said to his close friend Crito, just before he died:

> You will please me and mine and yourselves by taking good care of your own selves in whatever you do, even if you do not agree with me now. But if you neglect your own selves and are unwilling to live following the tracks, as it were, of what we have said now and on previous occasions, you will achieve nothing.

The thought is developed in several analogies that Plato deployed. For example, a potter will study pottery – its history, techniques and application but his real achievement will be in turning that knowledge into the production of excellent pots. A doctor will study medicine, learning about the workings of the body, the properties of medicines and the arts of healing but the purpose of this knowledge is to restore people to health. As the later philosopher Epictetus reminded his students, a builder does not offer to lecture on the wherewithal of building; he builds, thereby displaying his mastery of the art. Similarly, Socrates' philosophy suggested ways of caring for yourself – but the point was to do it, from discoursing with friends to contemplating death.

The paradoxical idea that knowing yourself was to comprehend something mysterious was picked up by the first Christians, though in a different way. Saint Augustine's autobiographical *Confessions* remains, to this day, one of the most profound attempts to see one's self clearly and without flinching. For Augustine, the best outcome of such a process is to realise your need of God. He tells the story of his life – and by implication any human life – as one that moves towards salvation: 'You have made us towards You,' he writes – the conclusion being that when someone understands the need they have of God, they will also have the conceptual tools they need to know themselves as well as they can. Like Socrates, Augustine keeps the difficulty of the task centre-stage: 'There is something of man that the spirit of man that is in him does not know.' We are strangers to ourselves, capable of endless self-deception in our desires and preoccupations. For Augustine only God can finally lift us out of this mire of delusion.

In the Enlightenment – the period of intellectual history in which human beings revolted against their limits and dependency on God – the idea of existential imponderability and impotence became objectionable. A variety of models for self-reflection were proposed that, while continuing to follow the injunction, did so in the hope that something certain can be ascertained. Sometimes this self-knowledge is fairly minimal: 'I think, therefore I am,' said Descartes, having doubted everything else that might be said about being human. According to other philosophers, knowing yourself was straightforwardly instrumental: we know that pleasure pleases and pain hurts, said the utilitarians, so let us not worry about the labyrinthine puzzles of interior speculation and simply pursue happiness. 'Let me consult my own passions and inclinations. In them must I read the dictates of nature, not in your frivolous discourses,' wrote David Hume, in similar mood.

The Romantics reacted against this pragmatic approach, arguing that pleasure for pleasure's sake itself makes people sick, like eating too many sweets. The word that is most closely associated with the attempts of Rousseau, Hölderlin and Wordsworth at knowing themselves would be 'authenticity'. Theirs was the struggle to recover a sense of oneness by plumbing the depths not of reason but of feeling. For Wordsworth, nature is the place where he discovered himself, via the power of his creative imagination: 'All / That I beheld respired with inward meaning.'

Later, Sartre proposed another variant on the Enlightenment theme. If human beings find a darkness at the centre of themselves, this is not because of anything that is mysterious or unknown; rather it is because there is nothing there: 'Nothingness haunts being,' he wrote. This emptiness might at first be thought alienating and threatening. Yet it is also an opportunity, since if there is nothing essential about being human, this makes for a tremendous freedom to be whatever you want. Though this freedom is also fearful: 'I am condemned to be free,' he added.

Not until Freud did what might be called a truly Socratic agenda return. For Socrates, the human condition was the source both of our uncertainties and our confused awareness of them. For Freud, the unconscious was the zone where that unease is manifest and from which fantasies and neuroses spring. The 'talking cure' is a practical skill, like the skills that the ancient philosopher learnt. The free associations of the analysand, coupled to the insights of the analyst, are aimed at understanding something of the self, in all its muddle. They provide a mirror to the self, if a cracked one. The aim is to develop a way of talking that provides a basis from which one is able to care more properly for oneself, though it is a risky business. We might perceive things, from Oedipal desires to death wishes, that do indeed make us want to run away and scream.

36

'Tell the truth but tell it slant. Success in circuit lies.'

Emily Dickinson

If you were going to start a new movement – nothing small, just an idea that could change the world – what would be the one practical thing essential for success? I suspect that it would be the genius technology we call the book.

Freud would soon have been branded mad without the chance to ponder his ideas at length in *The Interpretation of Dreams*. Marx would have been no more than a journalist without the weight of *Capital* sitting resolutely on the shelf. If a religious movement is more to your taste, look at L. Ron Hubbard. Scientology was nothing until he wrote about dianetics. The body of teaching and techniques he left – in books – now power the spread of his philosophy (admittedly helped by celebrity followers). Consider the genius of Joseph Smith, who not only founded the Church of the Latter Day Saints on the *Book of Mormon* but propagated a myth of its origins: it was written by Mormon in 400 CE and kept hidden on golden plates until Smith was guided to their resting place by the angel Moroni in 1823. Khalil Gibran would be nothing without *The Prophet* or Robert M. Pirsig without *Zen and the Art of Motorcycle Maintenance*.

So, it has always struck me as remarkable that three of the individuals behind the more significant of the world's ideological revolutions did not, as far as we know, write a single word; left not a scrap to inspire their followers. Why?

Siddhartha Gautama, now known as the Buddha, left discourses assembled posthumously by his disciples. But after his momentous meditation, sitting under the bodhi tree, when he first achieved nibbana – the conquering of pain that lay at the heart of his great idea – he thought he would withdraw from the world. It was only later that he felt the imperative to share his insight with others, though not by writing. He always declined when asked to define nibbana. No verbalisation would do. Karen Armstrong describes that impossibility:

> The Buddha was convinced that though nibbana was not a supernatural reality, it was a transcendent state because it lay beyond the capacities of those who had not achieved this inner awakening. There were no words to describe it, because our language is derived from the sense data of our unhappy existence, in which we cannot conceive of a life entirely devoid of ego. In purely mundane terms, nibbana was 'nothing', because it corresponded to no reality that we could recognise.

The Buddah's big idea could not be revealed in words (or, for that matter, hidden by them) but only shown in a life.

Socrates' big idea came to him later in life. He was an Athenian of notable integrity until the prophecy from Delphi propelled him from being good to being great. No one is wiser than Socrates, the god said; which Socrates knew must be wrong because he knew he knew nothing for sure. Then the key to his philosophy – his revolutionary thought – struck him: wisdom is not what you understand but is about understanding the limits of your knowledge, your character, your actions – your life.

This is why he refused to write. Words are a distraction from the real task; working on your life. They give rise to an illusion of insight, which may never be embodied. That is the hard part. Why? Reading works in the wrong direction: unlike a conversation, it does not emerge out of you but asks to be let into you. And usually it is too polite. When did a book complain as you tossed it to one side? Worse, if you follow a programme – prescriptions to transform your life – it may actually limit your capacity to change. The effort to follow the prescriptions becomes oppressive: you have no energy to work on yourself, what with all the following! In a similar vein, Socrates' pupil, Plato, feared that if he wrote philosophy, rather than discussing it with others, it would become a soulless, intellectual exercise. He was only persuaded to write his dialogues because people demanded it. The dialogue form was his compromise because, though written, it at least presents an interaction of real people, struggling with the implications in their lives of thought.

Jesus did write, though his words were only doodles in the sand. They disappeared as the wind swirled through the dirt. Unlike Saint Paul, who took up the missionary mantle after Jesus' death, he did not instruct his flock in letters. He did so by being with them.

He read some words, from the Hebrew scriptures, at least once, on the Sabbath in his home town. He stunned his audience by saying that the prophecy the words expressed was fulfilled in front of them, in him. So revolutionary was this idea that it became the centrepiece of Christian theology: not a book but Jesus himself was the Word. 'I have come that you might have life in all its fullness,' he summarised on another occasion. He lived agonisingly fully, to show others how to do so too.

Inevitably, the first Christians, like Saint Paul, wrote of their experience of Jesus. Like the writings about the Buddha and Socrates, we must be grateful that they did or the figures behind them would have disappeared in a gnostic mist: who now knows anything about Zoroaster? However, the Buddha devised a method for ensuring the words were not the last word on their subject, by insisting on striving after his esoteric state. Plato did the same by devising artful exchanges. The Christians wrote not one but four gospels so that no one should dominate: though clearly about the same event, in their details they routinely disagree. Jesus performs only seven miracles in the Gospel of John; in Matthew he does dozens. Jesus is crucified on different days, according to which account you read. Mark's Gospel does not even have a resurrection. More profoundly, they are clearly written for different purposes – Matthew to convince Jews, Luke Greeks, John for those with a taste for some philosophy.

It is as if the word on the page is deliberately designed to force the reader beyond to the Word who lived life in all its fullness. The differences are not there to be resolved, like disagreements between historical documents or treated with embarrassment, as if they undermine the message. They are there so that the story of a life might not hold the believer back from the embodied transformation of their life in life. What a tragedy it is, therefore, when the Bible is declared inerrant. Those who do so turn the good book into a golden calf.

Perhaps Mohammed had a better solution to this problem. He acknowledged that a book is a must but included instructions that it should only be chanted and even then only in its beautiful original language: it is not to be taken literally; the big idea is far greater than that. Though even that strategy can fail. If you have a truly enormous idea, mere mortals will almost inevitably not wrestle with it but reduce it to a more manageable size, in a book.

The truth is that a big idea is often not well served by literature: success in circuit lies. But if it can't live with it, it apparently can't live without it either.

37

Crowd: 'Yes, we are all individuals!'
Individual in crowd: 'I'm not!'

Monty Python's Life of Brian

In 1985, Nick Kamen took his stone-washed jeans off on television, revealing his toned torso and white boxers. It changed the world – or the world of advertisers. Kamen's sexy divestment, to the soul classic 'I Heard it through the Grapevine', was the centrepiece of the new Levi commercial, set in a 1950s laundromat. With it, the brand achieved a synthesis that all fashion labels long for. Levi jeans became at once a mass market item and a sign of their wearer's cool individuality.

The combination is, of course, a contradiction. How can a pair of denim trousers, virtually identical to those worn by billions, simultaneously carry the distinctiveness of a person's individual style? It might have something to do with the cloth, which moulds to the unique shape of a particular bum or thigh. It has much to do with the ability of Levi to load meaning onto minor differences in the cut of its jeans, creating a market for product lines from 501s to RedWire DLX. It all began with that advertisement, a trick that ad-land creatives have sought to repeat countless times.

What advertisers seek is a commercial that is so striking it hits the viewer as if it was meant for them and them alone. Another way of doing it, which has come on leaps and bounds since 1985, is encouraging the one-to-one advocacy of a product. Take 'viral marketing', email adverts that arrive in your inbox straight from a friend. Kraft, the manufacturer of the cheeses beloved by children, was an early winner at this game.

The problem Kraft had with marketing its 'lunchables' is that it is illegal to use, for marketing purposes, personal information about children under the age of fourteen. Lists of the names, addresses and preferences of this highly influential group of consumers simply cannot be bought. Viral marketing provided Kraft with a way around this impasse. The company did a deal with Pokemon to create a series of jointly branded digital postcards that kids could email to their pals. The postcards were a hit. Very soon, Kraft had tens of thousands of children exchanging its cards and it was receiving record brand exposure as a result.

Viral marketing has now morphed into 'buzz marketing'. It might also be called managed word-of-mouth advertising, the idea being to encourage existing networks of friends to talk about a product and thereby recommend it. Again, people then treat mass market items as if they were one-offs for them. For example, a teenager may be given a new pair of designer trainers before they appear in the shops, to enhance their desirability. Or a taxi-driver may be coached in how to describe a holiday destination, to talk it up in his cab.

Ethically, this is a minefield. Advocates say the techniques depend upon individuals being interested in the product to start with, so the advertising is only reacting to a choice already made. Detractors say it is manipulative and devious – the use and abuse of friendship. Underlying it is the question of whether the market forces that Nick Kamen so beautifully embodied enable us, as individuals, to be more ourselves in the consumer choices we make or whether they destroy our individuality by enticing us into acting with the herd. Rather like those who read the Harry Potter books because everyone else has and those who don't for the very same reason, thinkers on this conundrum can be divided into two camps.

There are those who think capitalism nurtures individuality by increasing choice. They argue that the brilliance of the modern economic system is that it converts people's innate creativity into wealth-generating processes. According to this view, any good idea can potentially be converted into a business that can, in turn, reach a receptive audience. The entrepreneur is happy with their success. The consumer is happy because they are able to access the original idea and incorporate it into their lifestyle and sense of self. Moreover, because capitalism, in theory, increases the wealth of everyone, it also provides everyone with more time and money to spend on these individuating activities. Recalling the *Life of Brian*: when the crowd shouts, 'Yes, we are all individuals', according to this line of thought they are absolutely right.

The other possibility is immediately raised by the solitary individual who shouts back, 'I'm not!' If everyone is wearing the same pair of jeans, eating the same cheese or enthusing about the same trainers or holiday – or following the same messiah – surely this is herd behaviour. As Lars Svendsen, author of *Fashion: A Philosophy* points out, fashion is impersonal by nature. It cannot supply us with the personal meaning we are striving for. The way fashion conceals this fact, Svendsen continues, is by making a fetish of the new. Almost as soon as it has been worn, a fashion item becomes superfluous, demanding the individual move on to the next thing. By forcing individuals continually to ask themselves what they think about what is new, fashion detracts from its deceit.

Another way of thinking about this is to consider the difference between a tradition and a lifestyle. After all, the debate might continue, people have always copied others; it is just that the copying used to be called tradition, whereas now we call it lifestyle. This, however, is not quite right. There is a crucial difference; a lifestyle is chosen. As a result of the power of consumer markets, one lifestyle can readily be replaced by another. A tradition is not so easily shifted; and it is not chosen, it is inherited.

A lifestyle might be thought preferable, for the very reason that it allows individual choice. However, the question is what is being chosen – in reality, one mass-market item after another. Worse, such lifestyle choices struggle to provide meaning, because there is no need to be committed to them, as you are to the things that make up a tradition. A lifestyle can be dropped as quickly as it can be adopted.

The danger of mass-marketed individuality is not only that you might, one day, walk into a restaurant wearing the same shirt as someone else. It is that a lifestyle is no more than a question of taste. In the extreme, ethics, the profound matter of how to live, is replaced by taste, the trivial choice of what to wear.

THE END OF LIFE

38

'In wonder all philosophy began. In wonder it ends.'

Coleridge

A couple of years ago, a northern bottlenose whale appeared in the River Thames in London. The sight and then plight, of the twenty-foot long beast from the deep – thrashing hopelessly in the tidal shallows beneath Westminster, Vauxhall and Battersea bridges – captured the imagination of the country. Twenty-four hour news programmes cleared the decks for uninterrupted coverage. Thousands of Londoners stood along the banks of the river to catch a sight of it. Later in the afternoon, the story took a twist. The body of a baby whale was found near Putney. Was our whale a mother, looking for her offspring, to protect it? The mood intensified. Commentators started recalling the death of Diana.

Vets and marine biologists debated the best course of action to save the struggling creature. Eventually it beached itself and, stilled, was winched on to a barge, cradled by pontoons and sprayed with water. Out in the air – its body weight collapsing its lungs and causing convulsions – it was rushed down-river to a place where it might be released to the open sea and saved.

The whale did not make it. At around 7 pm, it was reported to have died, after a final, desperate fit.

It was an extraordinary news day, reflected in the coverage that continued into the following week. Details of the autopsy were reported and so were theories as to why the story had been so big. But why? Was it just a slow news day? Or did the intimate sight of such a majestic, ancient animal make it so gripping? Was it the minute by minute portrayal of the selfless, human sympathy displayed by the rescuers? More darkly, was the rescue attempt symptomatic of guilt – guilt for the suffering we humans more commonly inflict on our fellow, sentient creatures?

I followed the story and found it amazing for one reason above all others. I thought of the whale itself, in an undifferentiated haze of panic, discomfort, pain and slipping consciousness – profoundly aware of its own distress but only cloudily perceiving the fearful kerfuffle around it. Was it like a horrid dream, when you can't escape because your legs won't work and you cannot comprehend why? I juxtaposed that experience with the human experience of the afternoon: the medical expertise of the vets who tended it; the technological wizardry of the television cameras that broadcast it; the millions of humans who peered, sighed and talked. What became so extraordinary was the thought of the radical difference between the whale's experience of its last hours and the experience of those who watched them unfold. The whale had absolutely and undeniably no concept whatsoever of the human world that had swung into action around it.

Perhaps, I thought – half in a dream myself – there are aliens with minds immeasurably superior to ours (in the haunting words of H. G. Wells) who watch out for us, tend our planet and save us from ourselves. Could we ever know whether there were such intelligences or not? Would their interventions be any more comprehensible or appreciable to us than ours were to the whale? No, I thought – perhaps a good idea for a short story but a route to madness as a conviction about reality.

Then I realised the reason why the difference between the whale's experience and our own so fascinated me. It had to do with the limits of what we know. We are like the whale, inasmuch as there are undoubtedly whole spheres of existence about which we are ignorant. But the difference between us and apparently all other creatures on the planet is that we know of our ignorance. That difference is what makes us human. Knowing we know little is the start of wonder and the beginning of philosophy.

39

'The optimist proclaims that we live in the best of all possible worlds; and the pessimist fears this is true.'

James Branch Cabell

World events provide every reason to be pessimistic. The crisis in the Middle East; the proliferation of nuclear powers. Even the sunshine portends global warming. Pessimism is usually thought to be a bad thing, leading to disillusion and resignation. 'I think of a pessimist as someone who is waiting for it to rain,' cried Leonard Cohen.

Is that right? Could it be that optimism is the cause of our problems, because it sets people up for disappointment and secretly fears that things will actually go wrong? Pessimism, on the other hand, could be the right attitude – morally right as well as factually accurate – because it liberates us from the relentless expectation of progress and finds energy in realism about the world. It seems like heresy to say so.

In his book, *Pessimism*, Joshua Foa Dienstag points out that a whole school of philosophers including Nietzsche, Schopenhauer and Rousseau have thought so. They variously argue that the optimism of inevitable progress grips people's imagination like linear time: as modern clocks and calendars steadily advance, the temptation is to think that human civilisation is also advancing. What actually happens is that this progressivism, like time, wears us down, causing disillusionment and resignation.

Pessimism is therefore different from nihilism, that wants nothing in life and even from scepticism, that knows nothing. Rather, it expects nothing but works at everything. Is it not the case that political heroes were often dissidents who had little or no realistic prospect of success but just knew they had to do something? This liberated them to act extraordinarily freely. The pessimist does not give up but quests – like Don Quixote – lightened by life's absurdities. Furthermore, they can see the wood for the trees, in confronting the evils on the doorstep and not being distracted by the distant horizon. Just a thought.

40

'Do I feel lucky? Well, do ya, punk?'

Callahan in Dirty Harry

There is a true story about an only child – a boy – whose father died just weeks after his conception. His mother became the centre of the child's life. People who saw it remarked, without hesitation, on the 'beautiful affection and worship' he lay before her. How devastating then was the day when, aged only three, the child was stolen, in an opportunistic raid, by gypsies.

The child's mother had taken him the few miles to visit an uncle, who lived in an old, though not especially remote, house on the banks of a blustery, coastal river. The boy took to playing outside the front door, apparently safe from danger. Until the gypsies passed by.

For a while he was not missed. Then his uncle noticed his absence. A frantic search began. Time was now passing quickly, for even on foot, gypsies could disappear like owls into the nearby wood. Then, luckily, his uncle received word that a tinker woman had been seen carrying a child, who was crying piteously. He gathered some neighbours and caught up with the child-snatchers a few miles away in the trees. Seeing them approach, the chief perpetrator of this inexcusable crime threw down her sobbing bundle and fled. She was never found. The child was returned, without hurt, to his distraught mother.

This incident is told by the biographers of Adam Smith, the famous philosopher of modern capitalism. As one of them comments, Smith would have made a poor gypsy, for he was a sickly child. However, his luck was in. Upon starting school a while later, his passion for books and extraordinary memory were quickly spotted. He became one of the most brilliant thinkers of his age. As one of the biographers reflected on the incident, luck became 'the happy instrument of pre-serving to the world a genius, which was destined, not only to extend the boundaries of science but to enlighten and reform the commercial policy of Europe'.

The rest of Adam Smith's life was a steady progress, with no fur-ther occasions when divine dice might have been heard rolling on the heavenly baize. It is startling that they could have fallen differently on that day. The piteous crying might not have been heard; the young child might not have cried but simply disappeared. But, then, of course, we would not have counted the tragedy as hideously unfortu-nate. We would simply not recall it at all.

Such logic underpins one response to luck: the more rational mind concludes that it is not anything real. Furthermore, it should not con-cern us, because too often it becomes enwrapped in superstition, with talk of starry fates and occult forces and things that are 'supposed to be'. Perhaps there is a minor sense in which people make their luck. Had Adam Smith's mother not loved her son so intensely, he might not have loved her enough to cry so piteously. You might, then, say her love was his luck: it saved him, becoming the sobs that were luckily heard: but no more.

Strictly speaking, luck merely qualifies an event – 'lucky' accentu-ating a positive, 'unlucky' a negative. So if the lottery numbers you picked on Friday match those that tumble out of the drum on Satur-day, the 'luck' is really coincidence, if a welcome one. If the cancer treatment a patient receives cures them, they are not actually blessed, though it feels like it: other factors, poorly understood, have put the patient into the percentile for whom the treatment works. If the fun-damental constants that describe the physics of the universe need only have shifted by a fraction of a fraction of a fraction for life to have been impossible, this also indicates nothing – according to this view. Had they not been as they are, we would not be as we are to notice.

Yet the concept of actual, naked, luck persists. It seems to capture something that is true, if unsettling, about life. Thinking that bad luck comes from putting boots on the table or the number thirteen does seem excessive. Yet you do not have to be David Hume – a contempor-ary of Smith – to suspect that there is a gap between cause and effect. Quantum mechanics has proven Hume right: it is impossible to say whether a particle will be here or there; you can only give a probabil-ity – and does that not sound a bit like luck? Similarly, you do not have

to be an expert in chaos theory to believe that forces beyond our comprehension, let alone our control, can have quite as much impact upon
a life as a butterfly's wing can have on weather in the tropics. There are
cases in which luck seems like as good a connecting thesis as any other.

The way the ancients entered into so elusive a subject is half-
remembered in our language to this day. They generally reckoned that
whether or not someone lived a good life had much to do with luck.
This is why the word happiness is, at root, very close to happenstance;
to be unhappy was to be hapless. They pointed to all sorts of factors in
life that had to be configured correctly for human excellence. It
started at birth and the need to be born with adequate capacities. A
person's upbringing and early experiences of friendship had to be
affirming, depending on all sorts of chances, from the socio-economic
status of their parents to whether their first impulse to share toys was
met with acceptance or rejection. Then there is the matter of education – and do not think, oh parent, that you can get that right with the
right choice of school. Educational success depends on indeter-
minable side-effects that cannot be pinned down, let alone planned.

Childhood, incidentally, is the period in which I was unlucky.
Aged about ten, I had put great effort into a primary school essay, I
think on the important subject of what I did at the weekend. I was desperate to know what my teacher thought of it and in class, fidgeted for
several days before he marked it. When he did, he informed me, with
a ghastly expression that still makes me shudder: 'Vernon, I have a
bone to pick with you.' I did not know what he meant. I am not sure he
did, upon reflection. But his meaning was clear: he did not like my
work. He'd probably just had a bad week. But for years afterwards, I
avoided writing whenever I could, opting for sciences and music.
Until, in my early twenties, I thought I had a vocation to be a priest
and studied theology. I was lucky – or was it God? – for, in writing
essays, I rediscovered the joy of composing sentences.

Having made the connection with serendipity, the ancients put a
lot of effort into finding ways around luck. Many attempted to store
up luck in heaven, by sacrificing to gods. Others were more philosophical. There is a story about Socrates walking out of a tragedy by
Euripides because in it, an augur had recommended letting happiness
happen haphazardly: 'That is absurd,' Socrates muttered, expressing
a remarkably modern sentiment and one that was taken very seriously
by at least one group of Socrates' followers, the Stoics. Everyone is

faced with a choice, they reasoned; the good life can be left to the random perturbations of uncontrollable factors that come from without or it can be shaped by factors that are in an individual's control because they come from within. The wise person cultivates the latter and when the former intrude – say, in calamities – they stoically carry on.

Euripides himself was far from as carefree as his augur character suggests. For tragedy is another response to luck; arguably the most profound. These heart-rending plays aimed to conjure up a direct experience of the painful, paralysing effects of luck on life. Take another of Euripides' works, *Iphigeneia at Aulis*. It tells the tale of Agamemnon's terrible luck when, waiting at Aulis to sail for Troy at the start of the Trojan War, the winds, strangely, failed. His assembled troops grow increasingly restless with the wait, psyched up with bloodlust for battle. He must move soon. Then a seer tells the king that the unfortunate weather stems from offence he has given to the goddess Artemis. He must sacrifice his daughter, Iphigeneia, in recompense. As the story unfolds, Agamemnon's agony, his wife's desperation, his daughter's distress and her betrothed's rage give life to the ill-fated suffering of great lives. The play does not aim to settle the question of who is to blame, though all parties receive blame at some point. Neither does it explain away the core conundrum, though all sorts of reasons are offered against and then in favour, of making the ghastly sacrifice. Rather, the tragedy allows the audience to identify with the characters in their extremity and so learn something about themselves and the world in which they live – a world that rests on so much luck. *Iphigeneia at Aulis* must have spoken particularly powerfully to the Athenians, because in the year it was first performed, 402 BCE, it won first prize at the Dionysia.

Tragedy offers a different interpretation of the impact luck makes on life. It does not try to avoid it, by appeasing gods; nor minimise it, by the exercise of reason. Rather, it suggests that the good life is one that is best able to cope with the ravages and the rewards of luck. The good person is one who comprehends the impact of luck, for good or ill, most profoundly. The good character is one that can admirably embrace it. This person is the hero of tragedy. Often they are the ones who suffer the most and in our sympathy for them we see their greatness. In *Iphigeneia at Aulis*, it is Iphigeneia who arguably wins this accolade. She, who has the most reason to rage against fortune, becomes quite tranquil as the inevitable approaches, finally offering herself for sacrifice. Her reward is to be replaced by a deer at the last minute, at the instigation of none other than Artemis. The gods were often thus moved by human heroism. It was a quality they could not show, not being subject to luck.

Which suggests one final observation. To be born with a silver spoon in your mouth is not, actually, to be born lucky. The philosopher Martha Nussbaum wrote a study entitled *The Fragility of Goodness* – the good being fragile but the fragile also often being good. She put it like this: 'Where there is the most luck there is the least insight.'

41

'I don't want to achieve immortality through my work ... I want to achieve it through not dying.'

Woody Allen

Who wants to live forever?

The question can be sung to a resigned melancholy, mourning the loss of something never known. It can be asked with a trace of bitterness – perhaps inflected with a truculent 'anyway': 'Who wants to live forever, anyway?' It can be posed in all earnestness, for example by the Chief Technology Officer of a Californian cryonics facility, assuming the answer: obviously, everybody.

Whether people would want eternal life, were they handed it on a plate, is debatable. One, strictly unscientific, Internet poll indicated that most would not. Many respondents were put off immortality because of the implication that it would necessitate more and more and more of the same – more joys and pleasures for sure but also more boredom and pain. They did not equate eternity with perfection. Conversely, the group of people in the poll who did eagerly anticipate everlasting life were those who saw it transformed after death, by God. Others testified that they did not hope for immortality because they believed they would reach a point in life when they had done all that they wanted to do and all they could do. They would then be content with an end. This is an interesting response, since it suggests something about the human condition. Although in theory there are any number of things to do in life, in practice any particular person can only take up so many, not because of time restrictions but because to be a person is to have limited capacities. We are like batteries; we become exhausted. Better, we are like the eyeless mole that lives in the dunes of the Namib Desert, thriving not in spite of our limits but because of them.

The wittiest reply to the poll was the person who said they did not want to live forever, so that they could see what happens next.

Philosophers provide reasons for finding satisfaction in either mortality or immortality according to whether they otherwise believe in the afterlife or not. One line of argument hangs on whether eternity adds meaning to life. Pascal thought that the question of immortality was of supreme importance and, believing the soul immortal, he argued that this life should be ethically oriented to the next: an immortal soul's unending existence renders its current temporary state trivial – apart from the impact now has on next. This, Pascal thought, is what gives life meaning. Putting it in more gentle terms, Thomas Aquinas took it that the greatest cause of happiness on Earth is the perception that life now is the start of a journey to perfect happiness in heaven. To deny immortality would be like being a mountaineer who only ever climbs halfway up the peak.

Those who doubt immortality contest that if meaning cannot be found now, it is meaningless to presume it would be found in a next life: if this life's meaning is found in its immortal version it begs the question of what it is about immortality that makes the difference. Not unendedness, since that is a measure of quantity not quality and it is quality that counts for meaning.

Then there is the matter of the nature of that eternity. It is famously addressed in a play, which later became an opera and an esteemed philosophical paper; *The Makropulos Case*, by Karel Capek. He told the story of a fabulous opera singer who is right at the top of her game. She is thirty-seven years old, though during the course of the plot it turns out that she has been thirty-seven for three hundred years. An elixir had been discovered by her father, Makropulos: one drop adds three hundred years to life. The play comes at the moment when she is debating whether to take a second dose.

The first three hundred years had, in certain ways, been marvellous, mostly because she was able to perfect her art and was likely never now to be surpassed. However, that perfection was achieved some while ago and as the centuries mounted, she had become frighteningly bored. Pointlessness, emptiness, meaninglessness, uselessness – vanity: these are the words that repeatedly come to her lips. The pursuit of excellence brought meaning. The excellence, once reached, wore thin.

Bernard Williams unpacked why in his philosophical paper about the play. He made two points. First, that for the singer's life to be meaningful, she had to remain recognisably the same person. Over a long period of time, let alone eternity, this is impossible. Think how difficult it is for people to cope with change even in the course of a normal lifetime. Then imagine being born in London in 1600. The population was around 150,000, the modern-day size of a pleasant, riverside market town such as Stratford upon Avon. Three hundred years later, the city is a sprawling metropolis of over seven million people. Admittedly, you would have had three hundred years to get used to it but Williams' point is that you would have had to become a different person to do so. If external change happened around the opera singer without also dramatically changing her, she would have been left either detached and mad or solipsistic and sad.

Second, Williams continued, some people might argue that she could transcend mortal change by becoming engrossed in her timeless art. Would not the same works be sung in 1600 as in 1900, with many more enriching compositions besides? She could lose herself in the music. However, to do that would be to become detached from herself again. Court renditions of William Byrd in 1600 would have become diva performances of Wagner by 1900: impoverished wench to Kiri Te Kanawa; it is inconceivable.

However, immortality cannot be dismissed because of the existential contortions it implies, for eternity does not just make its presence felt at the end of life but also in the midst of life. Consider a joy, like spending time with friends. Now ask a question: is remembering times spent with friends as good as the time itself? And if not, as seems pretty clear, then surely the remembrance is marred because the good times have passed. The anticipation of time with friends might be more joyful than the later recollection; the excitement of a visit being a greater joy than the satisfaction of even a good parting. In other words, remembrance portends a final separation; it is tinged by a desire for immortality. What is paradoxical about this remembrance is that it is itself a necessary part of friendship. How can you have a friend unless you have shared times with them in the past? If such loss is the flip-side of love, then the shadow of mortality is too.

Having said that, the desire to be happily reunited with family and friends in an afterlife is riddled with conundrums. If being happily reunited is predicated on being recognisably the same, then we come up against the problems posed by the Makropulos case. Believing that these problems can be solved by religious faith is no easy way out either. If before being reunited we are to be transformed by death – 'in a moment, in the twinkling of an eye, at the last trump: for the trumpet shall sound and the dead shall be raised incorruptible and we shall be changed' – it seems we shall not then be like the person we are now, the person whom those we know now love. And vice versa.

A mortal's contemplation of immortality is inevitably going to be like circling an event horizon and never seeing into the black hole. The concept of immortality definitely has something of the incomprehensible about it. It is its main characteristic. Note how it is spoken of in the negative. It is im-mortality, the prefix 'im' being a variant of 'in', from the Latin 'not'. There is nothing positive to be said about immortality, only that it is not like mortality – not dying, not sinful, not forgotten and so on. This could be taken as a failure of comprehension and imagination, the 'im' marking a metaphysical boundary that it is not possible to pass. Or it might be the best reason for trying to contemplate immortality.

Nietzsche showed why with a thought experiment. Imagine an everlasting existence that came with a single condition: you would have to repeat the same life in every detail again and again and again. This was his doctrine of the eternal recurrence. If it sounds strange, at least it sidesteps the dilemmas of Makropulos. Then ask yourself what difference that perspective makes on what you would do next, now, in this life. You would want to do something that you could welcome doing innumerable times. In other words the net effect of contemplating his version of immortality is to focus your attention most intently on the present. If you cannot decide what to do next under these imaginary conditions then it suggests that your present life is not as satisfying as it might be.

For most, the occasions on which an existence of eternal recurrence can be embraced with equanimity will be fleeting. It is not a comfortable thought. That, though, is the object of the exercise. No matter how impossible, contemplating immortality – at least from time to time – can sharpen your sense of life. Paradoxically it throws you on to the present. It deepens the sense of now. Conversely, to dismiss immortality because of atheistic convictions or to diminish its challenge in an easy expectancy born of religious faith, is to weaken its enlivening force. Only with an engaged scepticism can the mysteries of immortality give voice to the human condition. 'Death destroys a man: the idea of Death saves him,' wrote E. M. Forster.

42

'Truth rests with God alone and a little bit with me.'

Yiddish proverb

I used to be a priest in the Church of England. A few years later, I left, an atheist. Then, something else unexpected happened. I became a passionate agnostic. I realised that religions carry a wisdom that human beings cannot do without, though I was equally sure that I could not make the assertions of faith that modern church-going requires. The question, for me, became: how to be a committed agnostic? Can it be more than just a shrug of the shoulders? Is a spirituality based on art galleries and enjoying music enough? Can it add up to a way of life? I think it can: and moreover, that it matters.

Today, we live in a culture with what might be called a lust for certainty. Dogmatic science would have us believe that it has all the answers and can feed us body and soul. Religion, too, is being hijacked by a conservatism that turns 'faith seeking understanding' into statements of unquestioning belief. This matters, because many of the things that are going wrong in the world appear to stem from the resulting hubris – be that the aggravation of conflicts because of religious fundamentalism or the danger of environmental disaster because of technological Utopianism.

Agnosticism is an answer to that, because it rejects an equal and opposite militant secularism or Luddite technophobia. Daniel J. Boorstin put it well: 'I have observed that the world has suffered far less from ignorance than from pretensions to knowledge. It is not skeptics or explorers but fanatics and ideologues who menace decency and progress.' It is a passionate agnosticism that sees science as inspired by wonder, nurturing a piety towards the world. And it is a passionate agnosticism that understands the religious spirit not as the imposition of answers but as the pursuit of connections and questions. It is not just those disillusioned with dogmatic science and strident religion who seek how to be agnostic. Our future flourishing as human beings arguably demands it too.

At one level, I left the church because I became disillusioned by the antediluvian conflict over issues of sexuality and gender that grips it. But at a more profound level, I could not help but think that the church is too often remarkably unreligious. I do not mean that Christians are badly behaved which they may or may not be. Rather, it is that modern churches seem uninterested in the great quest that powers the spiritual life. Very often, the theology of the pew appears to be little more than the sophisticated assertion of certainties. The greatest goal of prayer is help finding a parking space at the supermarket. Worship is not an encounter with the unknown but a feel-good experience.

On the other hand, I stopped being an atheist because I came to think that its triumphalism entails a poverty of spirit that is detrimental to people's humanity. It tends to ignore or ridicule the 'big' questions of life – those questions that must be asked, if never conclusively answered. Having read all the arguments for and against, I came to think that whether or not God exists is an open question but that keeping it open, rather than trying to find a knockout blow one way or another, is the key.

This is what I mean by being a committed agnostic. T. H. Huxley, the Victorian 'Darwinian bulldog', invented the word to describe his position of neither asserting nor denying that for which there is not enough proof to do either. God is the supreme example of that. I think Huxley's definition is useful but reads rather dryly, so I am inspired, by two other figures, to re-inject some passion: Socrates and Saint Augustine. Socrates said that the key to wisdom is understanding the extent of your ignorance. He was agnostic in not asserting philosophical beliefs; instead, he went around ancient Athens asking awkward questions. Saint Augustine realised that human beings are 'between beasts and angels', as he put it. That is, to be human is to be ignorant of many things but is also to know that you are – to be ignorant but not pig-ignorant. To develop that sense is to deepen one's humanity.

A related reflection: the battle between science and religion is at best a cul-de-sac and at worse a dangerous self-indulgence. It is a cul-de-sac because arguing about whether God exists or not only goes round and round in circles. It is dangerous because in forcing people to take sides, it pushes them to fundamentalist extremes – based on religious or scientific dogma. What are genuinely fascinating, humanly enriching and socially essential are the places where science and religion meet. People like the evolutionary biologist and evangelical atheist, Richard Dawkins, try to decry such engagement, because it offends their faith that science can say it all.

The big challenge for the agnostic is whether agnosticism can add up to a philosophy of life, like religious belief or scientific materialism. Socrates is the key in this. His philosophy – his love of the wisdom he lacked – dominated his life. With reason, honesty, friends and questions, he pursued the Delphic injunction to 'know thyself'. Philosophy, for him, was only partly a matter of thinking clearly. More profoundly, it was a matter of transforming himself. Socrates was, crucially, religious, finding in god-talk the perfect reflection of human uncertainty, since matters divine are nothing if not ultimately unknown. Socrates' agnosticism provides the basis for a philosophy that puts reason's limits centre-stage and, even more importantly, inspires an ethos – a way of seeing the world – that can add up to a way of life. It is fascinated by the big questions of how to live and where to find meaning in life.

It suggests three things. First, meaning is not found directly; it does not come off-the-shelf. In this, it is rather like happiness. Second, you have to live – to live life in all its fullness, as it says in the Gospel of John. To turn to books, even well-reasoned ones and expect meaning to leap at you off the page is to turn to the abstract for that which has to be embodied. Third, you have to be fascinated by questions, not obsessed with answers, because that is what it is to be most fully human. This is, perhaps, like Keats' negative capability: 'When man is capable of being in uncertainties, mysteries, doubts without any irritable reaching after fact and reason.'

Index